The Way of Christ-likeness

The Way of Christ-likeness

Being Transformed by the Liturgies
of Lent, Holy Week and Easter

Michael Perham

CANTERBURY
PRESS
Norwich

First published in 2016 by the Canterbury Press Norwich
Editorial office
3rd Floor, Invicta House
108–114 Golden Lane
London EC1Y 0TG, UK

Canterbury Press is an imprint of Hymns Ancient & Modern Ltd
(a registered charity)
13A Hellesdon Park Road, Norwich,
Norfolk NR6 5DR, UK
www.canterburypress.co.uk

Hymns Ancient & Modern® is a registered trademark
of Hymns Ancient and Modern Ltd

British Library Cataloguing in Publication data

A catalogue record for this book is available
from the British Library

978 1 84825 901 0

Typeset by Manila Typesetting Company
Printed and bound by CPI Group (UK) Ltd

Contents

v

In thankfulness for Bishop Kenneth Stevenson
and in gratitude to the many communities
in which over the years I have celebrated
the liturgies of Lent, Holy Week and Easter

Foreword

For me Holy Week and Easter have long been important. Many years ago I came to believe that their celebration can change and transform individual lives and the lives of Christian communities. I learned that partly in the 1980s through having a part in the creation of the Church of England's services for this period of the year, but rather more as a leader of worship in a variety of settings and as a participant, a worshipper. Holy Week has been a significant contributor to my character and my response to life. I was able to write about the services and how to make them beautiful and effective in a book I wrote with Bishop Kenneth Stevenson published in 1986 as *Waiting for the Risen Christ*. I was able to write about the meaning of Holy Week some years later in a Lent book entitled *The Sorrowful Way*. Inevitably both those books are no longer available.

But I am grateful to SPCK for allowing me to use material from both of them in this new book and I am more than grateful to Canterbury Press for wanting to publish this new book, the majority of which is freshly written. Other people have written about Holy Week and its liturgy in the years since I last wrote about them, but they have focused either on the performance of the liturgy or on the significance of the story. Those that have addressed the liturgical questions have tended to be addressed more to churches with a catholic tradition, where a rich pattern in Holy Week is already established. I have wanted to speak more to those who have not yet found the way to take on board the rich provision now on offer and who are ready to explore a fresh approach. And I have wanted to explore the story and the liturgy together and to urge my central theme: that the story and the liturgy together can touch us deeply, change us and, in the words of the title of this book, allow us to find, however tentatively, the way of Christ-likeness.

Biblical quotations are all from the New Revised Standard Version of 1989. The hymns and songs are, except where otherwise noted, from *Ancient & Modern: Hymns and Songs for Refreshing Worship* (abbreviated to *A&M* in the text).

I

Introduction

A personal journey

Growing up within the Church of England I have some memories of Lent, Holy Week and Easter as a child might remember them. Lent was clearly about giving up things like sweets and chocolates. It could be about going to church more – my father got up earlier than usual on Fridays in Lent and went to Holy Communion before going off to work. It was a Lenten observance, if not a Lenten penance. I remember, of course, pancakes on Shrove Tuesday, but there was no ash to remember on Ash Wednesday.

In Holy Week there was a lot of church-going, but on Palm Sunday I recall only the giving of palm crosses. On Maundy Thursday a celebration of Holy Communion in the evening, making a particular impression because it was the only day in the year when there was an evening celebration. Good Friday meant a three-hour service, mainly preaching, and I particularly remember one year when the preacher dwelt on the physical pain of what Jesus suffered on the cross. Only the very pious stayed for three hours; most did one hour and then departed. In the afternoon we went out as a family to gather primroses and moss (it was legal then) for decorating the church for Easter. Then in the early evening there was a procession of witness, the five Anglican congregations converging on the Cenotaph in the town centre and in later years joined, I think, by other non-Anglican congregations. There would have been no point in marching through the town centre earlier in the day to catch the shoppers, for all the shops were closed all day.

I think there was nothing at St George's, our church, on Easter Eve, except decorating the church for Easter. There was nothing for me until I discovered something at one of the other churches in the town. What I discovered was one of three big discoveries about Holy Week that came to me during my teenage and young adult years. This first discovery, at St Mary's, the more 'high church' (as we used to say) church in the town, was of something called 'the Easter ceremonies'. I think I was aged about 13 or 14 and went with my grandmother. This service was, as I experienced it, esoteric and mysterious. I understood little of it and the picture that lodged most clearly in my mind was the large Easter Candle being plunged into the water of the font. I sensed that this liturgy carried rich levels of meaning, but I didn't feel there was a great sense of occasion. Certainly it wasn't a great gathering of the church community. There were no more than a couple of dozen people there. But it certainly set me wondering and wanting to know more. It introduced to me a sense of entering a mystery when liturgy is rich and meaningful. Even when you cannot understand it, it can communicate something profound.

I can put an exact date to the second discovery. It was Palm Sunday, 3 April 1966 and I was 18. I was on my way south from Yorkshire and I stayed on Saturday night in Peterborough and went to the cathedral next morning for the Palm Sunday liturgy. I don't remember all the detail. I remember palms in procession, plainsong sung by the cathedral choir, the singing of the Passion and the sunlight streaming on to the altar and the ministers. Again it was rich and mysterious, but above all else it was stunningly beautiful, such as took my breath away. I didn't talk to anyone. It wasn't a kind of conversion experience. It wasn't the first time I had had a deep experience of the reality of God. But it was for me a revelation of the beauty of holiness and ever since then I have wanted Holy Week to have about it a beauty that can touch people deeply.

I had to wait some years for the third discovery. There were some good experiences of Lent, Holy Week and Easter in between, but it was on Easter Eve, 29 March 1975, that I made the greatest discovery of the three. It was my first year at theological college and we all gathered in All Saints' Church Cuddesdon for the Easter Liturgy on the Saturday night, with the Bishop of Oxford, Kenneth Woollcombe, presiding. Here were the Easter ceremonies I had met before, but very different on this occasion. This was a major gathering of the community, not just something for those who like esoteric things. There were lots of symbols – fire and light, water, bread and wine – but, for all the sense of entering a mystery, their meaning was clear. The liturgy took us through Scripture, Baptism, Confirmation and Eucharist, with a wonderful sense that this was the night of Jesus Christ conquering death. Alleluias abounded and everything made sense. Above all there was joy, deep happiness. It was thrilling. I had a sense that it was changing me and others too. I had a further sense that it was this liturgy, the culmination of a week spent together from Palm Sunday till this point, that more than anything else formed and could transform this community.

As a priest it has always made me want to help people experience Holy Week and Easter in such a way that they can catch the experience I have had. I have wanted them to sense the mystery, the beauty and the joy. I have wanted them to be thrilled and to be touched. I have also wanted the common life of the churches in which I have worked to be transformed by celebrating Holy Week and Easter together as a community, not necessarily in one dramatic year, but over the years, going a little deeper every time. I tried to do that as a curate and then as a parish priest. Later I had the privilege of doing it in cathedrals, tapping into a rich tradition and renewing it where it was tired.

Meanwhile, a little way into my ordained ministry, I was invited into the Church of England's Liturgical Commission and I was part of it when, between 1981 and 1985, we worked on a new book, *Lent, Holy Week, Easter*, that was published in 1986. To be honest we had not expected huge sales. The Church was busy exploring *The Alternative Service Book 1980*, which had quite enough innovation for some people, and we expected *Lent, Holy Week, Easter* to interest only those with a fully developed liturgical life for that period of the year. However, the new book and its provisions did catch on remarkably and transformed the keeping of Holy Week in a very large number of church communities.

Those who wanted to understand more fully what these new services could offer needed a commentary on them and I wrote that in partnership with my friend, Kenneth Stevenson, then Chaplain of Manchester University, later Bishop of Portsmouth. Kenneth brought his considerable academic knowledge to the work and I tried to bring the skills of an imaginative parish priest, and we both brought our experience of working on the material in the Liturgical Commission. Our commentary, *Waiting for the Risen Christ*, is, unsurprisingly, now out of print, but I have tried to bring some of it into this book in order to share it with a new generation 30 years on. *Lent, Holy Week, Easter* is also out of print, but only because its provisions have nearly all been incorporated into the Church of England's *Common Worship: Times and Seasons*, and remain the Church's official provision for the days from Ash Wednesday to Pentecost.

It was during my time as a parish priest in Poole that something else very significant happened to me during Holy Week. This too has been fundamental in my understanding of the power of the liturgy of Holy Week to change lives. In 1992 my father, who lived 25 miles away from me in Dorchester, was dying of cancer. He was at home being cared for by my mother. It was touch and go whether he would make it to Easter. Through Holy Week and the first days of Easter I was going backwards and forwards between Poole and Dorchester leading the Holy Week services in my church and visiting my father. On Maundy Thursday I presided at the Eucharist of the Last Supper in the church and stayed for a while after for the Watch that we kept in the darkened church till midnight. People came and went, some stayed longer than others, but always there were those 'watching with Christ', sharing the Gethsemane experience. I didn't stay long, because I had the drive to Dorchester and, when I reached my parents' home, I continued the Watch, but now at my father's bedside. I was back in Poole and in the church in time to conclude the Watch there at midnight. It was, of course, all about making connections, the story of Jesus, the liturgy that celebrated the story and the personal experience all coming together in a deeply moving way.

Next day, Good Friday, I shared in all the liturgical celebrations in church which, of course, included the words of Jesus from the cross. I was struck by their brevity. They were exclamations more than sentences, cries for help or cries of accomplishment. How much it must have cost Jesus to speak as he hung there. Then I was on the road again to Dorchester to be with my father. He was quite distressed that afternoon, for he wanted to talk to me about his funeral, as it happened, in particular about his hope that some of his friends would play part of the Elgar string quartet. But he was having such difficulty in speaking. Communication was very difficult. Again I found myself making connections. Jesus struggling to say important things through the pain of the cross, my father struggling to say important things, despite the drugs to relieve his pain, as his death drew near.

I was able on Easter Day to bring Holy Communion to my father. Again there had been a sharing in the liturgy in church, with all its alleluias and its joy in the Risen Lord, and its meeting with Christ like the two who travelled on Easter evening to Emmaus. I was able to travel to Dorchester and enable him to share, for the last time on earth, in the Easter sacrament and perhaps to sense the presence of the Risen Christ in the room.

Making connections

You cannot, I believe, move from the liturgy to these 'real life' experiences without making connections, without seeing that in the experience of Christ is the experience of every person, and without seeing how a lifetime of trying to follow Christ in the way of the cross gives to those suffering and near to death resources that make them spiritually strong and able to face everything with a gentle, accepting faith. That, of course, is the ultimate walking in the way of the cross. We walk it only once for ourselves, but more often with others whom we love. But I am not saying that we keep Holy Week simply to prepare us to be strong in the face of death. We keep Holy Week to make us open, sensitive and faithful in all the testing experiences of human life, to help us make connections in all of them.

Many years later, when I became Bishop of Gloucester, I resolved to spend Holy Week each year in a different deanery or team or parish within the diocese, to walk with that congregation the Holy Week journey and, with the goodwill of the parish priest, to introduce a richer and more satisfying liturgical experience, with quite a lot of teaching to help people grasp what we were doing and why and how it might impact their lives. I was never disappointed, except sometimes that not as many people as I hoped came to share in the experience. Every time there were people who wrote to me afterwards and said how the experience had changed their life or deepened their faith or made them think afresh. Sometimes also the parish priest would report that this shared experience had been a turning point in the life of that congregation, not least in the number of people hearing a call to some new form of ministry.

One of the insights I gained from those weeks spent in deaneries, teams and parishes is how difficult it can be to bring congregations together in Holy Week, but how necessary it is if there is to be a critical mass for each of the celebrations and if those who plan the liturgy do not have to devise a full set of services for every church. There is a sensitive pastoral task, which may mean working patiently over several years, to convince congregations to come together in one place through the week-days of Holy Week and maybe at other times in Lent. But it is worth the effort if it is then possible to give people a richer experience. In Holy Week 2014, for instance, I was able to bring people together from a town and four surrounding vil-lages, with the principal liturgies in the town church, but with all four village churches being used during the week. Some of the same sort of bringing together may also be helpful across an urban set of parishes.

A Christ-like way

I have sometimes wondered how people understand the Church's call to celebrate Holy Week. I imagine that most consider it to be something we do in order to ensure that we do not forget. By retelling the story, by re-enacting it in some form or another, whether in the liturgy or through passion plays, we remind ourselves, not just of an awesome truth that Jesus died for us, but of the details of an extraordinarily powerful narrative. The more we do it the less likely we shall forget. In our own day, where knowledge of the story is poor outside the Christian community, the 'lest we forget' element is perhaps more about our culture and our society than about ourselves. People wear crosses without knowing why, even crosses with the figure of a man on them without knowing who he is or the story of his death and resurrection. We need to tell the story, for ourselves and for others, over and over again. It is part of the remember-ing to which Jesus called us.

But that is not all. I suppose we also keep Holy Week and celebrate Easter in order to engender and then to express grat-itude. We want to say the most profound of thanks to the God who in Jesus walked the Holy Week walk, hung upon the cross and burst from the tomb. Not surprisingly the official liturgies for Holy Week and Easter assume the setting of Holy

Communion, the place where Christians more than anywhere else say thank you. Gratitude, thanksgiving, is key.

Yet, as I have already indicated, that does not seem to me to be the ultimate reason. We celebrate Holy Week and Easter to become more like Jesus. To become more like Jesus, not just through a desire to be conformed to his pattern out of love for him, good reason as that is, but because to be like Jesus is to find the way to cope with all that life may throw at us.

To follow in Christ's way and be conformed to his pattern is not simply a matter of imitating his death, though it is in his passion that our identification with him is at its most formative. We enter into his mind, as far as we are able, in order to follow him through all the emotions of human existence. We share his joy, his faith, his easy relationship with his Father, his touches of humour, his capacity for friendship, his riding high, just as much as we identify with his need for space, his pain, his isolation, his doubt and, in the end, the fragility of his faith. The message of the Gospels is that the whole human story from birth to death and on to resurrection is a complex interweaving of all those aspects of human life. The way of the cross and the way of life and peace turn out, not so much to run in parallel, but to be a single path. To be conformed to his image is to enter imaginatively into his mind and heart and sometimes, as it were, even into his body.

I think it is important to say 'enter imaginatively'. Biblical scholarship has warned us against a foolish search for a kind of biographical picture of a historical Jesus of whom we can speak with confident detail. It is a legitimate approach to Scripture to use it imaginatively and creatively, to let its pictures interact with our own experience and our own longings, but we need to be wary lest we think we shall ever quite fathom the mind of Christ. Yet the story we tell of him – the words the Scriptures attribute to him (even when they almost contradict each other, as the words from the cross in the different Gospels very nearly do) and the images the Church has developed of him – engages with our story, in such a way that our own humanity becomes the more intelligible to us. In that revelation about ourselves we may know more of him and also of his Father. Through the story told of him we learn more of our own story. Through our own story, told with integrity, we perceive some of the truth about him, and even catch a glimpse of the divine.

This has always, I believe, been part of the Christian vocation. It is part of the timeless meaning of baptism. But there is a sense in which it may be more difficult in today's world for some people to make it their own. There has always been pain and suffering in the world and no one is quite exempt from it. In our contemporary world there is as much suffering as ever, and the record of the twentieth century was of evil, pain and suffering on a scale that undermined faith both in God and in the human race. Yet, for all that and despite the growth of terrorism that has come very close in the early years of the present century, we are more able in our Western culture to protect ourselves from some aspects of suffering than any civilization before us. We can alleviate pain in a way that has seldom happened before. We have created escape routes for many people from conditions of life that oppress and sadden and deaden, where in the past we would simply have endured. Fewer of us than in the past come face to face with death as part of normal existence. When we do come across it we are protected from some of its most shocking aspects. We see pain on our television screens perhaps more than we feel it in our bodies. Even our religious beliefs are more comfortable and less distressing than those of our forebears.

Much of that is good, but it may not help us to be conformed to the pattern of Christ that turns out to be the path of salvation. Although there are some Christians in our Western society who know exactly what it means to suffer with Christ, and even to go under when the suffering is intolerable, there are many whom life has treated so gently and smoothly that, almost guiltily, they cannot claim to walk in the way of the cross with any real knowledge of its weight and its cost. For much of my life I have known myself to be one of these. How may such people follow Christ with integrity and find themselves moulded into his shape?

I believe that one of the answers – and it is only one – is that they may be formed in their Christian discipleship and moulded into shape by the liturgy of the Church and in particular by the celebration of the Christian year, which is at its most compelling in the days before and during Easter. The celebration of the Christian year, in its succession of feasts and fasts and seasons, brings before us the story of Jesus. It places it within the context of worship in such a way that people may reflect and explore and, crucially, make connections between that story and their own, or between that story and the story of those who suffer today. In Holy Week especially, we can let our own experience of challenge, rejection, denial, desertion, pain and fear, as well as of joy, fellowship and integrity, interact with his. Bit by bit, year by year, we are enabled in retelling the story, through the words and songs and symbols of its annual cycle, to go a little deeper, to enter more profoundly into the mind of Christ. Though our assimilation of it may sometimes leap forward in a great bound, more often it is a gradual and almost imperceptible process of growing into Christ.

Within that process someone who has been going through a great trauma (whether bereavement or loss of faith or mental illness or criminal investigation or unrelenting physical pain) may be helped little by little to work it through, to discover a Christ-like way to respond to their trauma. Within that process somebody else who feels that their life is too easy and shallow may be given insight, by entering into the experience of Christ, to enter also into the sufferings of those around them in a way that they could not do before. Within that process another set of people may learn enough of the way of Christ that when, one day in the future, they are faced with a crisis unlike anything they have known before, their response will be instinctively Christ-like.

This Christ-like way is not, of course, a resilient rising above every trauma and crisis. But nor is it a kind of fatalistic going under in the face of loss or pain or fear. The way of Christ goes with events, not exactly rising above them or being dragged under by them, but going on being open and alive through them, patient and creative through them, integrity intact, even if faith sometimes fails. That is the pattern of Christ.

Year after year I have commended that view to congregations as I invited them to keep a holy Holy Week. I know that I often said that I hoped that, if some awful trauma came my way, I would be given the grace to live through it in something like this Christ-like way, not rising above, not going under, but keeping going with integrity and creativity. I have always been very wary of talking of some of the tests and irritations that mark our human lives as 'having our cross to bear'. People belittle the meaning of the cross by identifying it with the minor difficulties of life. But just occasionally something can come along that feels big and challenging enough to feel like a participation in the cross. Such a trauma hit me and my family in 2014 when an allegation was spread across the media, a process of investigation by the police and then the Church lasted ten months and I was excluded from ministry and lived under a cloud of suspicion in a sort of limbo. It was my *annus horribilis*. The question I found myself asking through that period was whether all that I had believed and taught about the Christ-like way did come to my rescue and enable me to keep faith with God and with myself. I believe that I can say that it did, though I shall be more cautious in the future about whether to speak of 'living creatively' through trauma. Patience and resilience seem nearer the mark. Easter Eve, with its waiting, as much as Good Friday, with its pain, is part of the story. But then comes Easter and the return of the alleluias.

It is out of experience that I commend this Christ-like path. If the remainder of this book focuses more on the celebration of the liturgy itself, so that it may reflect the mystery, the beauty, the joy and the power to change I encountered long ago, let it not be forgotten that this liturgical experience is, as well as celebrating the story of Jesus and being thankful, about finding the Christ-like path in which we may walk with patience, flourish and embrace life with integrity.

2

Lent

Origins

In these forty days you lead us into the desert of repentance that through a pilgrimage of prayer and discipline we may grow in grace and learn to be your people once again. Through fasting, prayer and acts of service you bring us back to your generous heart. Through study of your holy word you open our eyes to your presence in the world and free our hands to welcome others into the radiant splendour of your love. As we prepare to celebrate the Easter feast with joyful hearts and minds we bless you for your mercy. (*Times and Seasons*, p. 218)

Among the texts for Lent in the Church of England's *Common Worship*, these words set out clearly some of the major themes of Lent. Forty days, desert, repentance, discipline, fasting and prayer all have their place and each needs to be unpacked. There is a sense of movement. It is a pilgrimage towards Easter. In its origins it is one of the most complex of the Christian seasons.

In the popular mind Lent is about the time that Jesus spent in the wilderness. Among the Gospel writers, Mark expresses it most succinctly. The context is crucial. Jesus has just been baptized by John in the River Jordan and the Holy Spirit has descended on him like a dove.

And the Spirit immediately drove him out into the wilderness. He was in the wilderness for forty days, tempted by Satan; and he was with the wild beasts; and the angels waited on him. (Mark 1.12–13)

It happens at once, this entry into the wilderness, as soon as he has been baptized, and it does not happen at the instigation of the 'devil' whom Jesus will meet in the wilderness, but is the work of the Spirit who has just come upon Jesus in his baptism. That may indeed be a clue to the fact that wilderness experience is a good thing. The wilderness has the potential to be a place of encounter and revelation. 'Wilderness' recalls the place where the People of Israel were 'tested' for 40 years after their exodus from Egypt. Moses too had undergone a 40-day fast in the wilderness of Sinai (Deuteronomy 9.18) and Elijah a similar fast near Mount Horeb (1 Kings 19.8). Those were not times of temptation but times of testing, and 'tested' is a better word than 'tempted' for what happened to Jesus.

Matthew and Luke in their Gospels both elaborate the story and the element of testing in three particular tests. If Jesus is the Son of God, which is what he has been declared to be at his baptism, will he turn stones into bread, will he cast himself down from the temple, will he worship Satan? It is all about finding out what kind of Son of God Jesus is to be. The two writers differ over the order of the tests and introduce variations of their own. But the overall message of both is that Jesus emerges from the wilderness having passed the test, with his integrity and his relationship with the Father intact. The desert has turned out to be a place of growth and grace.

But is Lent all about these 40 days in the wilderness? English Christians have been much influenced by the nineteenth-century hymn, 'Forty days and forty nights' (A&M 121).

Forty days and forty nights
thou wast fasting in the wild;
forty days and forty nights
tempted, and yet undefiled.

Sunbeams scorching all the day;
chilly dew-drops nightly shed;
prowling beasts about thy way;
stones thy pillow, earth thy bed.

The 'giving up' that is part of popular culture in Lent, abstaining from particular foods, drink or other luxury, is seen as an echo of Jesus' own fasting in the wilderness, leaving him hungry and thirsty and vulnerable to the temptation to turn stones into bread at the end of the 40 days.

Yet it is striking that in the liturgy for Ash Wednesday, the first day of Lent, there is no mention in the introduction to the service of the time in the wilderness, and the Gospel reading is not the account of that wilderness experience (though it is read on the following Sunday). Furthermore in much of the scholarly writing of recent years a relationship of Lent to the wilderness story has been played down. Even the Introduction to the season in *Times and Seasons* makes little of it. The reason is that scholars and liturgists have wanted us to refocus and to see Lent, not as a season about the sojourn in the desert at the beginning of Jesus' ministry, but about the journey to the cross and the empty tomb at the end of it, and to do so in the company of those preparing for baptism at Easter. However, Paul Bradshaw and Maxwell Johnson have in *The Origins of Feasts, Fasts and Seasons in Early Christianity* shown us that in a season that is certainly complex the wilderness experience is very much part of the tradition. It is a matter of putting the emphasis as much on Lent as following Epiphany as upon Lent preceding Easter. There is evidence of a 40-day fast, for baptismal candidates, unrelated to Easter, following straight on from Epiphany (6 January), with its celebration of the Baptism of Christ, and also of a later fast, originally of less than 40 days, leading to Easter.

That is to express very simply an immensely complicated and fascinating story. It accounts for why we have a season that seems to relate in part to an event at the beginning of Jesus' ministry, but to be more about preparing for events at the end of it, that seems at first to be located in the desert, but that also has an element of journey and pilgrimage about it and, for the last two weeks at least, seems to be on the road to Jerusalem. Any attempt to tidy it up and locate it in one place or give it only one meaning is doomed. We need to enjoy the complexity and the different layers that make up twenty-first-century Lent.

Even any attempt to establish a 40-day season turns out to be more complex than it at first looks. If you count 40 days from Ash Wednesday you reach Day 40 on Palm Sunday. If you begin on the First Sunday of Lent, sometimes called Quadragesima (recognizing that Ash Wednesday and three days following are a later development), you reach Day 40 on Maundy Thursday. If you insist on going from Ash Wednesday to Easter Eve you have 46 days, but if you then take out the Sundays, because every Sunday celebrates the resurrection, you are back to 40. The truth is that '40 days' is not intended to be a precise time, but indicates the kind of length of the season, whether speaking of Moses in the Sinai desert or Jesus in the wilderness or the Church in Lent. Of the possibilities above, the one that the Church has most often acknowledged is a 40-day period from the First Sunday of Lent until Maundy Thursday, with the fast continuing until Easter through a time called the *Triduum*, about which more will be said. What is quite certain is that, although Sundays are indeed celebrations of the resurrection, they are not somehow out of Lent, but very much part of it and retain its character in worship.

Character

It is helpful next to explore the character of the season. We have already encountered desert, repentance, discipline, fasting and prayer as key to its observance. The same prayer speaks of preparing 'to celebrate the Easter feast with joyful hearts and minds'. Are 'joyful hearts and minds' to wait till Easter or are they also part of Lent? The prayer is ambiguous. George Herbert, the saintly priest and poet of the seventeenth century, spoke of Lent, not as a fast, but as a feast. 'Welcome, dear feast of Lent,' he wrote. People have often seen Lent as a dreary and dour season. They have either resented it and wished its

40 days over as fast as possible or, just a little more positively, they have seen it as a kind of purgatory through which we need to pass because of our rebellion and sin.

To speak of joy and of feast is to strike a different note. It is not about abandoning the old disciplines – the fasting, the prayer, the abstinence, the spiritual reading, the solemn music – of Lent as now inappropriate. We need them more than ever. An age where there is more food on the supermarket shelves than ever before needs to learn the wisdom of fasting. A world where we rush from one excitement to another, or one duty to another, needs space and silence that lead to prayer. A culture of indulgence needs abstinence. A society that has lost its moral certainties needs repentance. A generation that communicates by soundbites and texts needs spiritual reading. A Church that celebrates a friendly accessible compassionate God needs music that pulls us up short before the majesty and the holiness of God. A time of economic turmoil, of international instability and of fears for the planet needs fasting, prayer, abstinence, penitence and much more in generous measure.

But there is joy. It lies, not in escaping the old disciplines, but in embracing them. The feast is the fast. Lent is one of those seasons that turn the conventions of the world upside down. Praying and fasting and all the other things begin to have their effect quite quickly. Within days, let alone weeks, we can sense that we are less enslaved to the material, more in touch with the spiritual, healthier, more alive and alert, more sensitive, more human. All that comes from the time-honoured disciplines. We begin to feel good and it is the disciplines that are getting us there. The fast begins to feel like a feast.

This may be the moment to remind ourselves of the baptismal origins of Lent. Even if it is complex, we can say with quite a lot of certainty that the post-Epiphany fast was in preparation for baptism and that, perhaps from a little later, but very much still today in some traditions, the pre-Easter fast was and is focused on preparation for baptism. The adult candidates for baptism underwent long preparation, two years perhaps of instruction and formation, getting them ready for the great moment when they would go down into the water, be anointed, be joined to the Church and share in the Eucharist for the first time. And when those two years were up, the candidates changed gear and entered a period of 40 days of real rigorous spiritual training for the momentous day.

Alongside the baptismal candidates there was another set of people keeping what we now call Lent. These were the people who had been excluded for a while from the sacraments because of some serious or scandalous sin. They had been, as we would put it, excommunicated, as a penance. In some communities they were to be readmitted to communion on Maundy Thursday or at Easter. They too went through these days of real rigorous spiritual training for the welcome day when they would return to the eucharistic fold. To express a complex process simply, in course of time other people came to see that it would be spiritually beneficial to all Christians to keep the 40 days alongside the candidates and the penitents. By this time it was a dynamic season, a journey to the cross and the resurrection, a kind of pilgrimage, keeping up with Christ as he set his face resolutely towards Jerusalem.

Although the testing in the desert remains an element of our keeping of Lent, ultimately the Lent story is not a wilderness story, but a journey. It is the story of Jesus walking with his cross until he comes to Calvary, though to get there we may well walk through the desert and find it a strangely purifying place to be. The Lent invitation is not to stand still for too long in the wilderness, but to try to keep up with Jesus as he walks resolutely towards that goal. All the way he walks, not with a glum face like one who goes to his doom, but with the joy of the one who does the Father's will and who knows that the cross will become a source of life and peace. He walks with a lightness in his step – more feast than fast.

There is a problem for us in joining this journey. The problem is sin. How can we walk joyfully behind or beside Jesus, or even trap him in conversation, or tell him that we love him and would give our lives for him, when sin gets in the way? The principal outcome we are looking for in Lent is growth – growth in faith, growth in discipleship, growth in wisdom, growth in Christ-likeness, growth in love of God and one another and, in a particular sense, of self. That is what God wants to bring about in us through the Lenten pilgrimage. Growth, more than penitence, but penitence is the pre-condition to growth. I believe it is right to describe the whole of Lent as a penitential season. We need more than a single day to examine our lives, confess our sins and move on. Nevertheless there is a sense in which the first day of Lent, Ash Wednesday, is the principal penitential day in the Christian year, when we so focus on our sin and our sorrow for it. The hope is that, although it continues to work its way through in the weeks of Lent, already we are leaving behind the weight of our sin and our failure, with all their negativity and alienation, and are indeed learning to be God's people once again. As the weeks of Lent go by, it is growth that God wants to see in us and we want to see in ourselves.

In *Waiting for the Risen Christ*, Kenneth Stevenson referred readers to the writings of Leo the Great in the fifth century.

Among the many preachers of antiquity, the one who stands out as a remarkable witness to Lent as a means of spiritual growth for *all* Christians is Leo the Great. Apart from fasting, but no doubt as a result of it, the ordinary Christian can 'scrutinize himself, and search severely his inmost heart; let him see that no discord cling there, no wrong desire be harboured'. Lent, however, does not end in soul-searching, however agonizing Leo's recommendations might become. The faithful should look to their neighbours: 'Let us rejoice in the replenishment of the poor, whom our bounty has satisfied. Let us delight in the clothing of those whose nakedness we have covered with needful raiment.' Apart from such works of mercy, Leo asks his hearers to abstain from wantonness, drunkenness, the lusts of the flesh, and much besides.

For he is convinced that 'it is by such observances . . . that God's mercy will be gained, the charge of sin wiped out, and the adorable Easter festival doubly kept'. (p.21)

Growth is the key. The very name, Lent, is derived from 'lengthening', the lengthening of days in springtime. It is a reminder that we, like nature, are to grow. There's a beautiful prayer I came across more than 40 years ago by Dick Williams in *Godthoughts*.

As the days lengthen and the earth spends longer in the light of day grant that I may spend longer in the light of your presence, O Lord. And may those seeds of your Word, which have been long buried within me, grow, like everything around us, into love for you and love for people; to become a visible declaration of your Lordship in my life. Grant, Father, that this Lent may be a springtime for my life in Christ.

Fast

The deepest Christian tradition about Lent is to keep it as a fast. It may be so joyful a fast that it takes on the character of a feast, but it is a fast nevertheless. It obviously means much more than abstinence from sugar, sweets or alcohol, and certainly its motive is not simply to lose weight, though embracing a healthy lifestyle is partly a spiritual matter. There has been a tendency in the Church in recent decades to discourage 'giving up' and to encourage 'taking up', taking on something new for the period of Lent. That, of course, can be part of the springtime growth and it may fulfil the words of the prayer that spoke of 'acts of service', 'study of [God's] holy word' and having 'hands to welcome others into the radiant splendour of [God's] love'. But that prayer does put fasting before all else. It is time to explore fasting a little more.

The Prayer after Communion on the Second Sunday of Lent prays that God will 'keep us both outwardly in our bodies and inwardly in our souls'. There is a proper balance there and we are right to keep that balance and not to become solely concerned about either body or soul. It goes on to pray 'that we may be defended from all adversities which may happen to the body' as well as 'from all evil thoughts which may assault and hurt the soul'. The age in which we live is a mass of contradictions. Part of that contradiction is that an age that probably abuses the body more than many before it in recent history – in terms of excessive food and drink, smoking and drugs, let alone sexual indulgence – is also more concerned with health and fitness than any recent generation. You might expect that an age in which there is so much affluence, at least in the West, with a higher standard of living for the majority than most would have dreamed of a generation or two ago (though appalling poverty for a minority), would see the need more clearly for a return to simple ways. In other words, in an age like our own you might hope that fasting and abstinence might have a place.

To talk of Lent as a fast is not to say that we should be giving up eating altogether. The evidence is that, if we did, most of us would probably still be alive at Easter, but not in the best state for keeping the Easter feast. We have the picture of Jesus in the wilderness resisting all food, living out the conviction that we do not live by bread alone. But the Church has never advocated total abstinence from food for ordinary Christian people going about their daily living through Lent. By the Lenten fast we mean something that falls considerably short of total abstinence. But we do mean sufficient simplicity of life, eating and drinking included, that the special spirit of the season becomes real for us, and the contrast with festival time significant and striking. The traditional 'giving up' is an expression of that, the sacrifice of luxuries, not because they are necessarily bad, but partly because reliance on them *is* bad, and partly also because, for Lent to feel quite different, there has to be a difference through every area of our life.

Traditionally a fast has meant giving up meat, though not many nowadays interpret a Lenten fast like that. Meat was chosen, not because it was particularly bad for you, but because it was seen as a luxury and a treat. Perhaps we do not see it like that today, though for some the Sunday roast remains the culinary high point of the week. Some of us are vegetarians, an increasing number. Nearly all of us are less reliant on meat as part of our diet than in the recent past.

But, if the point of the fast is to achieve a simplicity of life-style, then, whether it be meat or other things, the change from our usual pattern needs to be sufficiently great that we actually notice the difference. In the Bible and in the Christian tradition, the emphasis in fasting is placed on the good it will do to you, the one who fasts, rather than on any benefits elsewhere. But there is also, running through the Scriptures, a call for justice in which all the hungry are fed. 'He has filled the hungry with good things and sent the rich away empty,' sings Mary in her Magnificat (Luke 1.53). Scripture often makes a connection between the fasting of the 'haves' and the feeding of the 'have nots'. Isaiah underlines this when he has God say:

> Is not this the fast that I choose: to loose the bonds of injustice, to undo the thongs of the yoke, to let the oppressed go free, and to break every yoke? Is it not to share your bread with the hungry, and bring the homeless poor into your house; when you see the naked, to cover them? (Isaiah 58.6f.)

We need to be clear. It would do us good to fast (if we are in good health), even if there were no poverty or starvation in the world. But, given that there is poverty and starvation, it becomes part of our moral duty to ensure that what we save through abstinence relieves others, and does not simply find its way back into our pocket to pay, for instance, for our summer holiday. Fasting and giving go together in our world and the sense of physical well-being that comes from the discipline of fasting will equip us the better for those other parts of the Lent challenge – the 'acts of service', the 'study of [God's] holy word' and having 'hands to welcome others into the radiant splendour of [God's] love'.

The fasting or 'giving up' that becomes part of personal discipline in Lent needs to be reflected in the church building and in the liturgy. People coming into the church on Ash Wednesday need to be struck by the fact that they are walking into a space that has changed and become a more austere place. The change in liturgical colour (to one of the many shades of purple or perhaps to unbleached linen) will signify that. The altar table 'dressed' only in a linen cloth exposing the wood or stone is another possibility. The removal of brightly coloured banners adds to the austerity. The absence of flowers makes much the same point. Restraint in the use of music (perhaps, if voices are strong enough, unaccompanied singing) has its place. It is not, of course, that music or colour are wrong, but that contrast signals a change in mood, and the contrast on Easter Day when it all returns will be greater still. Avoiding a predictable sameness about worship is always desirable. What is true for Ash Wednesday remains true for all the days of Lent.

Liturgy

The simplicity and restraint of music and the texts that go with it traditionally include the omission of the Gloria at the Eucharist (except on the rare feast days that can fall in Lent) and the singing of one particular word. A long tradition of the Church in the West banishes alleluias through Lent, whether spoken or sung, in order that they burst forth afresh at Easter. There is a beautiful eleventh-century hymn in the older hymn books, 'Alleluia, dulce carmen', to be sung just before Lent that expresses why alleluias are banished in Lent. It is a pity that newer English hymn books have not provided a more contemporary version for use on the Sunday before Lent. But *The Hymnal* of the Episcopal Church has a version which includes these verses:

Alleluia though we cherish
and would chant for evermore
alleluia in our singing,
let us for a while give o'er,
as our Saviour in his fasting
pleasures of the world forbore.

Therefore in our hymns we pray thee,
grant us, blessed Trinity,
at the last to keep thine Easter
with thy faithful saints on high;
there to thee for ever singing
alleluia joyfully.

There is good liturgical teaching there.

The liturgy of Ash Wednesday, the first day of Lent, is fully explored in the following chapter. Much of what is written there about the character and mood of Lent applies in the weeks that follow. On the Sundays in Lent it may be appropriate to give more time than in the rest of the year to the penitential part of worship, and *Common Worship* provides a rich variety of texts with which to do this. It also provides Gospel acclamations, introductions to the Peace, eucharistic prefaces and blessings to enable the distinctive nature of the season to be maintained. But it is worth repeating that, however austere, Lent worship should never be dreary. At least part of its function is to encourage life and growth and even in Lent Sundays celebrate the resurrection.

Weekdays in Lent may also bring people together more often than at other times of the year, sometimes for house groups, sometimes for Bible study, sometimes for ecumenical activity, sometimes for worship. Some people will value the opportunity for a weekday celebration of Holy Communion. Some appreciate the late evening service of Night Prayer or Compline, perhaps at the end of another activity. *Common Worship: Daily Prayer* provides not only an order for Night Prayer, but also seasonal variations to make it more fit for purpose in Lent.

There is also the opportunity to explore the Way of the Cross through a series of 'stations'. *Times and Seasons* (pp. 236ff.) provides a brief history of the stations and a series of texts. In origin the stations were a pilgrim liturgy along the holy sites in Jerusalem. The number of stations has varied, but from the eighteenth century there have been usually been 14, though contemporary forms, including that in *Times and Seasons*, add a fifteenth, commemorating the resurrection. Some churches permanently have pictorial representations around the walls; others are in a position to place such stations in the church for Lent. In the end, pictures are not necessary; each station can be described or quietly imagined without necessarily having a visual image. A note in *Times and Seasons* also suggests that the stations can be represented symbolically. It suggests that the Agony in the Garden could be represented by a goblet or chalice filled with wine, the arrest of Jesus by a pair of handcuffs, and so on. This devotion is wonderfully flexible in the way it may be used – in one place or on the move, a handful of the stations on any one occasion or all of them, a free-standing devotion or part of a larger liturgy, a service rich in Scripture and liturgical text or a service of silences punctuated by minimal text.

The Fourth Sunday in Lent has acquired several names. Sometimes *Laetare* Sunday (from the opening word of the old entrance chant, 'Rejoice'), sometimes Refreshment Sunday, more often Mothering Sunday. *Times and Seasons* explains the connection between them in this way.

The Fourth Sunday of Lent (*Laetare* or Refreshment Sunday) was allowed as a day of relief from the rigour of Lent, and the Feast of the Annunciation almost always falls in Lent; these breaks from austerity are the background to the modern observance of Mothering Sunday on the Fourth Sunday of Lent (p. 211).

A sense of a slight let up mid-Lent is well established. Liturgically just a few churches have rose coloured vestments and hangings used only on this day and on Advent 3. The pastoral issue is always how far to let go of Lent to make the most of Mothering Sunday, a day on which many churches can reach out effectively into the wider community, resisting its decline into a secular 'Mothers' Day'. The loss lies in a break to the momentum of Lent and possibly some of the most powerful Lenten Gospel readings – the man born blind (John 9.1–41) in Year A and the 'Prodigal Son' (Luke 15.1–3, 11b–32) in Year C. The gain is in engaging with people coming to church especially for Mothering Sunday. *New Patterns for Worship* provides liturgical material to supplement the Mothering Sunday Collect, Readings and Post Communion in *Common Worship*. The Gospel readings, though both about Mary the mother of Jesus, retain the connection with the cross, with either Simeon's prophecy that a sword will pierce Mary's soul or Jesus' words to his mother from the cross.

In the end it is a pastoral judgement that has to be made in each community. It is always a sensitive area. Not everybody still has a mother. Not every woman who wants to be is a mother. Some mothers have lost a child. Some families do not reflect the traditional family of mother, father and child. Not that Mothering Sunday is intended to be all about our own mothers. Traditionally three themes have been held together – the Church as our mother, Mary the mother of Jesus and our own mothers. In the contemporary context some would want to explore also the motherhood of God or, reflecting Julian of Norwich, Jesus as our mother. Yet others will want to stay very clearly with the provision for the Fourth Sunday of Lent.

The Fifth Sunday of Lent introduces a new stratum. It is still Lent, but *Common Worship* tells us that 'Passiontide begins' and there are new liturgical texts for use from this Sunday. Behind the name lies a degree of confusion. Until the twentieth-century reforms the Roman Catholic Church kept a two-week Passiontide beginning on the Fifth Sunday of Lent, and named that day 'Passion Sunday', differentiating it from 'Palm Sunday' a week later. In its reforms after the Second Vatican Council, a two-week Passiontide was abandoned, the Fifth Sunday of Lent was simply called that and the name 'Passion Sunday' was attached to Palm Sunday at the beginning of Holy Week.

In the Church of England no Sunday is formally called 'Passion Sunday'. The Book of Common Prayer does not use the term, nor does *Common Worship*. All that the service books do is to indicate a change of gear from Lent 5, going deeper into the mystery of Christ's passion through the texts provided. There is no special ceremony for Lent 5. For some reason the unofficial name 'Passion Sunday', referring to Lent 5, continues to be used in many churches. Passion Sunday or not, Passiontide begins and its first week is an opportunity to be ready, rather than unprepared, for Palm Sunday and Holy Week.

There is a custom in a few churches of veiling crosses, crucifixes, statues, icons and other artefacts in church through Passiontide (in some places throughout Lent). People have found it odd that at the very time we are most focused on the cross we should cover it. But the origin lies not so much in covering the cross as in covering bright gold, silver and jewelled artefacts, whether a cross or not, in order to add to the plainness of the building and the liturgy. There was also a sense that, if the cross were veiled through Passiontide, the unveiling of it in the liturgy on Good Friday made all the more impact. Views will differ on the effectiveness of veiling, but, if it is done, it is important that the shape and outline of the cross is not lost, only the sparkle and the decoration. Purple and unbleached linen drapes can also be used in ways other than veiling to enhance the setting of the liturgy in Passiontide.

So for 40 or more days Christians are invited both to explore what it means to be in the desert and, please God, finding it to be not just a place of testing but a place of growth and grace, and also to be on a journey that is moving steadfastly towards Jerusalem and the events that changed the world and have the potential to transform the lives of those who share the journey. It is a good place to be and a good journey that begins on Ash Wednesday.

3

Ash Wednesday

Liturgy

> I invite . . . you in the name of the Church, to the obser-
> vance of a holy Lent, by self-examination and repentance; by
> prayer, fasting, and self-denial; and by reading and meditat-
> ing on God's holy word. (*Times and Seasons*, p. 223)

With this text the president at the Ash Wednesday liturgy
invites people to share the Lenten journey, and it is time to
explore the liturgy for the first day of Lent. It was the first service produced in 1986 in *Lent, Holy Week, Easter*. In a slightly
enriched form it is to be found from pages 221 to 235 in *Times
and Seasons*. Its intention is to provide a service of such effectiveness that people will be inspired to share in worship on
Ash Wednesday and experience the change of mood it brings.
Every effort needs to be made to celebrate Ash Wednesday in
every Christian community. Transferring every principal feast
and fast to the nearest Sunday leads to a loss in the distinctive emphasis of the celebration. Nevertheless a note (p. 222)
allows a pastoral decision to move this liturgy to the following
Sunday, the First in Lent.

The service is set within the familiar pattern of the Eucharist,
but with a Liturgy of Penitence and the imposition of ashes
between the Liturgy of the Word and the Liturgy of the
Sacrament. It would be possible to take the distinctive part of
the service out of its eucharistic setting, but there would be loss

in that. The Church may give us ash at the beginning of Lent, but God continues to give us bread for the journey.

The choice of hymns and songs for this celebration is important if it is to catch the mood of the day. It is a day of penitence – hymns like 'Dear Lord and Father of mankind' (A&M 621) would make sense. It is the beginning of a desert journey – 'Guide me, O thou great redeemer, pilgrim through this barren land' (A&M 652) or other hymns of pilgrimage would fit well. We need to call down the Holy Spirit to accompany us – 'Come down, O love divine' (A&M 238), not least because of its reference to 'dust and ashes'. We are beginning to look to Holy Week and to Easter – so a song that looks to the passion is appropriate. There are two fine new texts specifically for Ash Wednesday. 'From ashes to ashes' (A&M 122) is a song by Teresa Brown. 'From ashes to the living font' (A&M 123) is a hymn by Alan Hommerding. There are also good responsorial versions of Psalm 51, not least 'Have mercy on us, Lord' (The New English Hymnal, 532). Just a few churches would have the musical resources to sing the Lent Prose, 'Hear us, O Lord, have mercy upon us' (The New English Hymnal, 507). The music on this day needs to be quiet, reflective and restrained, but not dreary and not concerned only with one of the many layers of meaning of Lent.

The special nature of this day might be marked by the ministers entering in silence and the liturgy beginning without music, though a hymn or song is not inappropriate. The president greets the people and introduces the service with its call to repentance and to 'the observance of a holy Lent'. It is a careful text, though clearly the president is free to improvise. The response to it is the *Trisagion* ('Holy God, holy and strong, holy and immortal, have mercy upon us') or could be the *Kyrie eleison* or any short penitential song or chant; and the invitation to silent prayer and the Collect follow. So the Gathering part of the service is quite brief and terse, intentionally so.

The Liturgy of the Word follows in its usual form, allowing a maximum of three readings, a psalm and an acclamation (without an alleluia) before the Gospel, with the possibility, as always, of hymns, chants and songs. The two Old Testament readings provided as alternatives, Joel 2.1–2, 12–17 and Isaiah 58.1–12, both capture the mood of Ash Wednesday. A reading from the prophets feels appropriate. If there are to be only two readings, there is a case for one of these rather than that from 2 Corinthians. Perhaps more importantly Psalm 51 is sufficiently crucial a text on this day that it ought to be used, perhaps said quietly, even in communities that do not often use psalmody at the Eucharist. The sermon, because it leads directly into the Liturgy of Penitence, clearly needs to prepare the community for what is about to happen.

There follows a Liturgy of Penitence unique to Ash Wednesday. It consists of six elements.

- An invitation.
- A litany, penitential in tone.
- A period of silence.
- A confession.
- The blessing and imposition of ashes.
- An absolution or other concluding prayer.

The invitation is simply an invitation to 'call to mind our sin and the infinite mercy of God'. There is no instruction about posture but, in places where kneeling is possible and appropriate, this is certainly a moment when such a posture enhances the mood and intention, with the ministers themselves kneeling before the altar table. The two litanies, which are alternatives, allow solemn words to carry deep emotions. They may be sung or said as appropriate. A note directs that the silence at this point should be no mere pause, but a significant time of stillness. It is the time for each person to bring into their mind the sin and failure they want to lay aside. Some words by the president earlier in the service or perhaps in the sermon will have alerted people to the purpose of this time of silence. The spoken confession, richer in words and imagery than that in regular use, then allows that sense of sorrow and penitence to be articulated.

The blessing and imposition of ashes now follows. Although an optional part of the rite, it has been warmly welcomed and much used in churches of all traditions. The use of ash on this day goes back to about the ninth century, though it fell into disuse in the Church of England at the Reformation. The majority of churches have returned to it only since 1986. The blessing prayer prays that the ashes 'may be for us a sign of penitence and a symbol of our mortality'.

There is a tradition of making the ash from the palm crosses of the previous year, brought to church and burned before Lent. Or, where a church has used branches for the Palm Sunday procession, a few of them can be saved, stored, dried out and burned for the same purpose. In the end the source of the ash is not very important. Sometimes mixing the ash with just a little water to make a paste enables the mark on the forehead to be more distinct and cross-like. The president, if (s)he has been kneeling, stands to bless the ash in a bowl, receives the mark of the ash on the forehead from another person (a sign that this ministry is from one sinner to another), and then begins to do the same for the congregation, Where there are many people present others will also take bowls and trace the ash on the foreheads of all who are willing to receive this ministry.

The rubrics do not specify whether the people come to the minister, or the minister to them, for the imposition of the ashes, nor do they specify posture. Local circumstances will dictate what is best. In most traditional settings, it will be appropriate for the congregation to come forward, but perhaps to adopt a different posture from that at the distribution of communion. In other smaller and less formal settings, where people sit in a circle or semi-circle, the minister may come to them. With his or her thumb, the minister makes the sign of the cross in ash on the forehead of each. This may all be done with no words at all, but the words provided – 'Remember that you are dust, and to dust you shall return. Turn away from sin and be faithful to

Christ' – are appropriate and powerful. In the Roman rite these two sentences are alternatives, but here they are held together, the one rightly negative, the other positive, and both should be used together. It is better to have more ministers than fewer words. There may be singing or other music while the imposition is happening, but silence is also appropriate.

The Liturgy of Penitence concludes with a prayer for forgiveness, though it is optional, for there is a sense in which the imposition of ashes has provided a natural climax for this distinctive part of the service and more words might seem superfluous. Where a prayer is used, the first is more a prayer for strength than an assurance of pardon. Its use would emphasize the character of Lent in which the spirit of penitence expressed in this service is carried forward through 40 days of spiritual exercise. But a conventional absolution is also provided for those who believe that should be the invariable response to confession.

The ministers need then to wash their hands before sharing the Peace. The ash may remain in a prominent place for the rest of the service. The liturgy now picks up the ordinary flow of the Eucharist with the Greeting of Peace introduced with its distinctive Lent text.

Bread and wine are brought to the altar table. The Eucharistic Prayer is best with the extended preface with which this chapter began. The Lord's Prayer is given a distinctive introduction ('Lord Jesus, remember us in your kingdom and teach us to pray') and the less frequently used words at the breaking of the bread ('Every time we eat this bread and drink this cup we proclaim the Lord's death until he comes') is preferred. Both these texts would appropriately continue through Lent. There is a congregational Prayer after Communion different from the usual provision and then a Responsory and a short Dismissal Gospel before the Solemn Blessing and Dismissal. If all this material is used, there will be a case in some settings for a movement by the ministers to a place near the door during the singing of a hymn or song and for the Responsory, Dismissal

Gospel, Blessing and Dismissal to be at the door. This could also be one of those occasions when there is no music after the service, the liturgy ending in silence, just as it began.

Ash

In relation to Ash Wednesday, it remains only to reflect a little more on the meaning of the ash. From experience as a priest and a bishop I can affirm how strangely moving it is on Ash Wednesday going along the lines of Christian people standing or kneeling to receive the imposition of ashes. 'Imposition of ashes' sounds rather grand, but the reality is different. It is a powerful little moment of sheer simplicity, yet deep intensity. There are ancient furrowed brows on which the sign of the cross is made. There are the faces of the young, slightly embarrassed, lining up to be 'ashed' for the first time perhaps. There are eyes that are tightly closed, eyes wide open, eyes full of pain, eyes with deep joy. There are those haunting words: 'Remember that you are dust, and to dust you shall return.'

They are, at least at first, uncomfortable words that the minister says as the cross is traced on each person. It seems a hard saying, a reminder that in the midst of life we are in death; and for many it conjures up a memory of a graveside and those haunting words: 'earth to earth, ashes to ashes, dust to dust'.

'Remember that you are dust.' It is, first of all, an invitation to humility. It is easy for many of us to grow in our sense of self-importance, whether at work, or at church, or in organizations to which we belong, or even in our assessment of our place in our family. There is, of course, a strand of self-esteem that is necessary to our health and well-being, but equally there is a self-regard that can be an insidious sort of sin. 'Remember that you are dust' is a timely reminder, putting us gently in our place. It is not that we are insignificant. You cannot be insignificant when God loves you. You exist, you are, you have your being, because God created you out of the dust of the ground.

You are, you continue to be, because you are enfolded in God's love. To be reminded of one's mortality is, in the end, a positive, not a negative thing, for it is to have one's relationship with God affirmed. Though I am but dust, I live, I move, I have my being, because God loves me. It is a wonderful truth. It may prick the bubble of my self-importance, but it also affirms my eternal value in the eyes of God.

It reminds me also of my heavenly destiny. Yes, my body will return to the dust from which it came. Yet, because God loves me, I shall not perish with my flesh and bones, but will be lifted up to the One who first loved me into life and will draw me into immortality. When that will be, I can never know, but Lent is always an invitation to be ready and prepared. So in the dust, the ash, and in the stern words, 'Remember that you are dust, and to dust you shall return,' Christian people, as they begin the season of Lent, are reminded of the need for humility, assured of God's love that gives them breath, and pointed towards the immortality God longs to give them.

The ashes are to be a sign of penitence also. As the ash is traced on the forehead, the minister adds, 'Turn away from sin and be faithful to Christ.' This is not very different from the Lord's first proclamation when he comes into Galilee when John is baptizing, 'Repent, and believe in the good news' (Mark 1.15). By penitence we mean a real self-knowledge – What am I really like? How do I look to God? What is the truth about me? It is a self-knowledge that leads into sorrow, spending very little time in guiltiness or pity, and converts into resolution, a firm intention of amendment, another fresh start in God's generous world of new beginnings. The dust, the ash and the gracious call, 'Turn away from sin and be faithful to Christ,' strengthen in each one of us the self-knowledge that leads to sorrow, and the sorrow that is translated into resolution.

So Christian people on Ash Wednesday accept the cross of ash traced on their forehead. It is not an extravagant public humiliation. The Hebrew Scriptures are full of folk sitting publicly in ashes, wearing sackcloth, covering their heads in dust.

God is often portrayed seeing through it all, and dismissing it as worthless. One of the Gospel readings of Ash Wednesday itself warns against parading our prayer and fasting.

> Whenever you fast, do not look dismal, like the hypocrites, for they disfigure their faces so as to show others that they are fasting. Truly I tell you, they have received their reward. But when you fast, put oil on your head and wash your face, so that your fasting may be seen not by others but by your Father who is in secret. (Matthew 6.16–18)

What Christians do on Ash Wednesday is anything but extravagant, essentially restrained, hardly public in what it leaves on the forehead once the dust has settled. It is an acting out in gesture what lips, in words, and hearts, in silence, have been trying to express: a recognition of mortality, which is a sobering insight, and an expression of penitence, which is the crucial first step in the path of amendment of life. In the end the cross of ash is for every aspect of our humanity – for heart and mind and soul. Yet there is an appropriateness that it is on the body that the ash is traced, not only because it is that body that will return to the dust, but also because, in the spiritual struggle, it is often the body that lets us down. There is a self-indulgence of the heart and mind, but it is a self-indulgence of the body, whether in greed or sloth or lust, that often undermines our highest resolutions. 'The spirit indeed is willing, but the flesh is weak' (Matthew 26.41).

It is the sign of the cross that is marked on the forehead. It is not, of course, the first time that the cross has been traced there. For, when new Christians come to baptism, they are signed with the cross, the sign that inspires them to confess the faith of Christ crucified. The cross on Ash Wednesday is a reminder of baptism. Whether in the innocence of childhood or in the ardour of adult commitment, we received in baptism God's grace for the Christian pilgrimage. That pilgrimage goes on being a struggle, so often an upward climb, but we are engaged in it still, thankful for that grace without which the struggling would have been long since lost. Symbolically, on Ash Wednesday, we put the cross back, in ash this time as we recognize our failure, but the cross nevertheless.

Yet the cross on our foreheads points in another direction too. It looks back to our baptism, but forward to Holy Week. For in Lent Christians seek to understand more clearly what it means not only to be 'signed with the cross', but also to 'take up the cross'. There is on Ash Wednesday a looking back to our baptism in water, but there is also the forward thrust to Calvary, to be baptized with the baptism with which Jesus is baptized. This is the Lent vocation and the cross of ash brings both the looking back and the looking forward into one focus.

The looking forward is to Calvary, but it is also a looking beyond that to Easter. The Christian does not pretend through Lent that there is no light at the end of the tunnel. The Christian lives always in the power of the resurrection, even in a solemn season of penitence. On Ash Wednesday we may employ cold ash, rescued from a fire long dead, but in the liturgy at Easter we shall gather around a new fire, burning brightly, hot and red, giving warmth. From it we shall light the paschal candle, the sign of the Risen Christ into whom the Father has breathed new life. If, as we contemplate our mortality and our sinfulness, we seem like the coldest ash left in the long-untended grate, we need to remember that God has the will and the power to breathe new life into the least promising of embers and to kindle in the coldest heart the burning fire of love.

Nevertheless it is not only ash that is given on Ash Wednesday, but, as at every Eucharist, bread also. God does not give us ash when we ask for bread. We may not be worthy to receive even the crumbs from under God's table, but, as the Book of Common Prayer put it, his property, his character, 'is always to have mercy'. And so, sinners as we are, he gives us bread. Not the bread of this world's physical hunger, for Lent reminds us that we do not live by bread alone, but the bread, the sustenance, of his holy word, the word 'that proceeds from the mouth of God', and the bread also of the Eucharist, 'bread of angels' who ministered to Jesus in the 40 desert days. The Church gives us ash, a sign of reconciliation. God gives us bread, the banquet for those who have been reconciled, and he gives it again and again.

On Ash Wednesday we learn and take heart from the ash, but also from the bread, and begin to walk again with the cross once more traced upon our forehead and in our soul. For the invitation as Lent begins is always this: to come, in humility, penitence and confidence, and to turn to the Lord, who wipes the dust from our brow and places on our lips and in our heart the bread of heaven and the wine to make us glad again.

4

Holy Week

Origins

The week of Christ's passion is, for any Christian wanting to walk with Jesus, a demanding time. The reality in many church communities is that some will arrive in church on Easter Day to celebrate the resurrection having not taken part in any of the community's worship during the previous seven days. There are others who will have been in church on Palm Sunday but will not return for seven days, some others who may have found time to come for an hour on Good Friday. Yet a serious engagement requires that people spend some time each day, reliving with Jesus the events of that week. Some with full diaries and work and family commitments, if they are to do that, will have to content themselves with some prayer, Bible study and reflection at home or on their way to work. But the ideal that does need advocating is to clear the diary of all that is not necessary and be able to share day by day in the worship the Church can offer. We should not be afraid to ask a lot of people in this one week of the year, not least because it has so much to give them. Nevertheless there is a danger of over-load and each church needs to reflect on what is realistic if people are to make this Holy Week journey together.

The origins of Holy Week are, of course, complex. We know that in the earliest centuries Christians celebrated the passion, death and resurrection of Jesus in one long liturgy through the night and into the morning of Easter Day. There were no separate celebrations for what we now call Palm Sunday, Maundy

Thursday and Good Friday. It is not surprising that, when special liturgies on these days did emerge, it was in the city of Jerusalem, where the events could be relived in the very places where they first happened. We get a fascinating insight into this in the travel diary of a nun named Egeria who spent several memorable Lents, Holy Weeks and Easters in Jerusalem between 381 and 384 (*Egeria's Travels*). Egeria records quite a lot of detail of the liturgies in which she shares, inevitably writing more about the things that were novel for her than the things that were familiar back home in France or Spain. We shall note some of her insights in the following chapters.

In *Waiting for the Risen Christ* Kenneth Stevenson described the kind of piety Egeria encountered in Jerusalem as 'rememorative', because, he wrote, 'it is at root historical in its approach and its services are meant to remind the worshippers of certain "events", in order to build up their religious experience' (p. 4).

On the Sunday we call Palm Sunday Egeria took part in a procession down the Mount of Olives. On Wednesday a liturgy celebrated Judas' pact with the authorities to betray Jesus. On Thursday there is a commemoration of the Last Supper. On Friday there is a veneration of the cross. Here are the germs of the later Holy Week. It reads like one long play, made up of many acts and scenes. There is even a slightly relentless feel to the entire week. The services keep drama to a minimum. There is no donkey on the journey from the Mount of Olives and no re-enactment of the crucifixion. The 'events' are allowed to speak for themselves. 'The message is subtly suggested, not hammered home. The "events" are called to mind, but are celebrated in liturgy's truest form, a symbolic code,' Stevenson wrote (p. 5).

This raises immediately an important missional question. A subtle symbolic liturgy assumes a community that has some knowledge of the story and its context. But sometimes the story needs to be told in places where people lack that kind of knowledge. The way of the cross needs sharing as part of the task of evangelization. That requires a less subtle approach. Drama and re-enactment need to be employed. In medieval times this approach, which Kenneth Stevenson calls 'representational', took over. He mentions, for instance, the medieval mini-drama in the Easter liturgy in which robed ministers act the parts of the women at the tomb. In our contemporary situation it leads to donkeys on Palm Sunday morning and street plays on Good Friday. It is profitable to reflect on the difference between the 'rememorative' and the 'representational' when planning the keeping of Holy Week, the first engaging the church, the second reaching out into the secular culture.

Past made present

'Rememorative' is a liturgist's word for a particular approach to worship. Perhaps closer to people's everyday experience is to speak of 'reliving' an event. It is helpful to go back to the Jewish people of the time of Jesus and their annual commemoration of the Passover and the Exodus from Egypt. When each year the festival came round, they relived that experience, not as the mere recalling of something significant that had happened to their ancestors long ago, but as an experience through which they themselves were going. So powerful was this for them that it was, in reality, the making present of a past event. But it was the making present of a past event in the knowledge that a past event is simply a pin-pointing in time of an eternal truth.

Or look at the Christian Eucharist, not just in Holy Week, but at any time. We talk of Jesus giving us his body and his blood and we recognize his presence in our midst. Again this is the making present of a past event, in the knowledge that a past event is a pin-pointing in time of an eternal truth. The key word in the Greek is *anamnesis*, which we translate as 'remember', but it cannot be said too often and too loudly that our idea of remembrance is much weaker than this exciting experience of the past drawn into the present.

We need to hold this idea, that the past is made present and is found to reflect an eternal truth, in mind for a moment. Alongside it we need to put a second truth that we have already noted: that in Holy Week Jesus experienced a catalogue of emotions – popularity, anger, fellowship, love, fear, betrayal and more – that turn out to be the same kind of emotions that we experience in the ups and downs of human life. And then we add a third. It is the same truth from another angle.

There is a human need, one that most will recognize, to share, to talk about, to recite over and over again, particular events and experiences that have made a mark upon us. 'Do you remember the day we . . .' or 'I shall never forget the way I found him . . .' We do it especially with death. We go over the details, often with those who know them already, because we are not simply conveying information, nor are we simply remembering, in the sense of being careful not to forget. We do it because this recitation, this repetition, brings clarity and insight. Talking about it, talking it through, brings reconciliation and acceptance. It is part of the process of wholeness and healing.

These three affirmations – the past is made present and is found to reflect eternal truth, the experience of Jesus is the experience of every person, the rehearsal of past events brings insight and healing – together give the rationale of Holy Week. Like the Jew at the Passover, I hear how God acted, in Jesus long ago, but know it to be an account of how he acts in every person in every age, and know it to be how he acts in me today. Holy Week becomes this week. Jesus becomes me. And in that exercise I learn to understand myself, my lot, my destiny, God's role for me, God's care for me. As a human being I grow, please God, in maturity.

That is why the Church invites Christian people to enter as deeply and seriously as they can into the experience of Holy Week in preparation for the celebration of Easter. Holy Week is, as noted above, like a drama with several acts and scenes, or, perhaps better, like a great symphony, with its several movements each with its distinctive mood. You can listen to one movement of a symphony and find it attractive. But, if you want to enter into what the composer is trying to convey, if you want to be gripped by the music and be thrilled or touched by it, you need to hear it all.

The symphony of Holy Week has four great movements and the following chapters explore them in turn – Palm Sunday and the entry into Jerusalem, Maundy Thursday and the supper and the betrayal, Good Friday and the final walk to the cross, then Easter, with the empty tomb and the meeting with the Risen Lord. There may be other stories to recall and possibly other liturgical events to mark them. But these four are what matter. They are the four great movements of the symphony.

Monday, Tuesday, Wednesday

Yet there are also the three days between Palm Sunday and Maundy Thursday. There are stories relating to those days. The Gospel accounts vary somewhat in how they treat these days. Where they are consistent is that Jesus spends the day time in Jerusalem, the night time in Bethany outside the city. Matthew and Luke have him cleansing the temple on Palm Sunday after the triumphal entry, but Mark places this on Monday. (John has had Jesus cleanse the temple at the beginning of his ministry.) The Gospels all have Jesus teaching and Matthew places a huge body of teaching material in the temple between Monday and Thursday. Each Gospel also records an anointing of Jesus by a woman, though Luke has placed it earlier in his Gospel, John on the day before Palm Sunday, and only Matthew and Mark locate it within Holy Week. John identifies the woman as Mary, the sister of Lazarus and Martha. These three days also have accounts of the plotting and the plan for Judas to betray Jesus.

These three days have been variously used down the ages. Egeria describes them in detail. She records how Monday had a special service in the afternoon. On Tuesday, late in the evening, there was another special service which concluded with the long reading of Matthew's farewell discourse (Matthew 24.1–26.2), which ended with the flat statement that the Son of Man is to be handed over to be crucified. Wednesday ended even more dramatically with the reading of a narrative of the betrayal (Matthew 26.3-16) and Egeria added: 'The people groan and lament at this reading in a way that would make you weep to hear them.'

How are these three days to be observed today? In some communities they should not be observed at all if it means that people will not stay the course through till Easter. But, in places where it can be sustained, a service each day will enable people to come together as they move through the events of the week.

Cleansing, anointing, teaching and plotting are all themes that can be developed. The Gospel readings focus on three of these, all three drawing on John's Gospel, with the anointing by Mary on Monday, Jesus talking with the Greeks who wanted to see him and speaking about his death on Tuesday and Judas' betrayal on Wednesday.

There are five possible liturgical forms that can be used on these three days. One possibility is the use of Night Prayer, with the Gospel reading of the day, an address and the specific Passiontide material for Night Prayer. A second is some use of the Stations of the Cross (discussed in Chapter 2), but perhaps on these days it is better to focus on the events earlier in the week, saving the final walk to the cross for the Passion readings on Sunday and Friday.

A third possibility is the medieval office of *Tenebrae*, focused on the gradual extinguishing of candles. It ceased to be part of the Roman Catholic provision in 1955, but has seen something of a revival, not least among Anglicans looking for a powerful visual liturgy that expresses the growing darkness of Holy Week. Benjamin Gordon-Taylor and Simon Jones describe it fully in *Celebrating Christ's Victory*, though it is not to be found in *Times and Seasons*.

Nor does *Times and Seasons* provide for the possibility of an *agape*, which is strange given that it had a place in the predecessor of *Times and Seasons*, the volume *Lent, Holy Week, Easter*, which says this about it:

> *Agape* is strictly the New Testament word for love. It was also applied to a fellowship meal or love feast which, in the early Church, often occurred in association with the Eucharist. This was common enough in the second to fourth centuries, as is shown by references in the writings of Ignatius and Tertullian. But it created problems of discipline and fell into disuse. The last reference is in a Council of 692.
>
> Jesus enjoyed regular table fellowship with his disciples (Luke 13.26), and the sharing of a meal together has remained a sign of the intimate fellowship inseparable from true Christian discipleship. But the *agape* as a distinctive Christian celebration must retain its connection with the Eucharist. It is this connection which provides the *agape* with any validity it may have in the modern age. (*Lent, Holy Week, Easter*, p. 97)

Lent, Holy Week, Easter sets out how the Eucharist can be set within an informal meal. It envisages a celebration with people seated around the table with elements of the Eucharist interspersed between courses. It does need very careful planning and the fact that it died out in church history warns us of how it can be difficult and divisive. There are churches that have chosen to make their Maundy Thursday liturgy an *agape* meal. In Chapter 6 I will argue against that, but an *agape* earlier in the week, whether combined with the Eucharist or not, might well lead to a deepening experience of the meaning of the Eucharist of the Last Supper when it is celebrated on Maundy Thursday evening.

The fifth possibility on these three days and perhaps the most obvious, even though it is not part of the earliest traditions, is a simple Eucharist each day, with the use of the Scriptures provided, more than the usual amount of silence and the Eucharistic Prayer that keeps bringing people back to the cross and the passion.

5

Palm Sunday

Scripture

The name for the Sixth Sunday of Lent is important. Most calendars call it 'Palm Sunday'. As has been said already, the Roman Catholic Church now calls it 'Passion Sunday'. Both are right. Both together point to a truth. It is, in effect, 'Palm Sunday of the Passion'. It has its own story of Jesus' entry into Jerusalem, the 'Palm Gospel', but it is also the Sunday of the Passion, not just in the sense that traditionally the Passion as told by Matthew, Mark or Luke is read, but also in that it is the guarantee that those who can only come to church on Sundays do not find themselves reaching Easter without hearing the account of the trial and death of Jesus. This chapter proceeds on the basis that those who arrange worship on Palm Sunday will find a way of holding the two, palm and Passion, together and not for only one, more likely the palm story, to be emphasized at the expense of the other, for it is the Sunday of the Passion. The tension between the two themes is not a historical accident or a liturgical nightmare, nor is it just a confusion of ideas.

All four Gospel writers give an account of the entry into Jerusalem. They each have their variants and, as usual, John is the most distinctive. In Mark two disciples are sent by Jesus to a nearby village to find a colt. They are questioned as they untie it to bring it to Jesus, but are allowed to take it.

Then they brought the colt to Jesus and threw their cloaks on it; and he sat on it. Many people spread their cloaks on the road, and others spread leafy branches that they had cut in the fields. Then those who went ahead and those who followed were shouting, 'Hosanna! Blessed is the one who comes in the name of the Lord! Blessed is the coming kingdom of our ancestor David! Hosanna in the highest heaven!' (Mark 11.7–10)

In Matthew they bring both a donkey and a colt. Matthew, like John, draws on the words of Zechariah.

Shout aloud, O daughter Jerusalem! Lo, your king comes to you; triumphant and victorious is he, humble and riding on a donkey, on a colt, the foal of a donkey. (Zechariah 9.9)

All the accounts mention cloaks. Luke does not mention branches, but he does tell us that it all happens as they descend from the Mount of Olives. He has the disciples alone praising God, but he is more specific about the kingship of Christ. 'Blessed is the king who comes in the name of the Lord!' he has them exclaim (Luke 19.38). John places the initiative for the whole event with the crowd. Indeed the disciples initially fail to understand what it all means. It is Jesus himself who finds the donkey, and only in response to the palm-waving crowds. In John it is branches of palm trees they wave, not simply 'leafy branches' as in Mark.

Three of the four Gospels end with a strong but varied final word. In Matthew and in John it is the crowd who speak. Matthew has 'Who is this? . . . The prophet Jesus from Nazareth in Galilee' (Matthew 21.10–11) and John has 'The world has gone after him' (John 12.19). In Luke Jesus has the last word, 'if these [disciples] were silent, the stones would shout out' (Luke 19.40). The use of the different accounts in different years enables people to hear these variations, some of which are theologically significant.

Kingship

It is worth pausing for a short time on this concept of kingship. Zechariah, whom Matthew and John quote, speaks of the king who is coming, 'triumphant and victorious, humble and riding on a donkey'. We have grown accustomed to celebrating the kingship of Christ around Ascension Day or the Feast of Christ the King, but it is the Palm Sunday entry into Jerusalem that tells us most about this kingship. The words from Zechariah, the branches and, perhaps above all, the cloaks spread along the route like a red carpet, all point that way. So does the anointing of Jesus like a king that the Gospel writers place at this time and, in John's case, on the eve of the entry into Jerusalem.

Yet there was in the life of Jesus an ambivalence about kingship. When Jesus came to John on the bank of the Jordan the voice had been heard and the Father had claimed him as his own. 'You are my Son, the Beloved' (Mark 1.11) was what they heard from the cloud, and every Jew knew that, in terms of the Hebrew Scriptures, these were the words of God to the king, to David's heir and descendant. The baptism was the first anointing, the recognition of the crown prince, who would eventually enter into his kingdom in the holy city. But that first time, on the banks of the Jordan, there was no crowd laying down their cloaks and no triumphal procession. Rather, the young man fled, puzzled, into a desert place, there to be tested and to think through the destiny beginning to dawn upon him. There was no easy acceptance of the role or title of a king. Later, when the great multitude has been fed with loaves and fishes, John tells us that Jesus 'realized that they were about to come and take him by force to make him king' and 'withdrew again to the mountain by himself' (John 6.15). Jesus shies away from the kingship that they offer. Nevertheless on Palm Sunday his acceptance seems total, for he finds a young donkey and sits upon it, knowing that the crowds will recall Zechariah's words. It is a clear acceptance of the kingdom.

What has happened? What has changed? Why does he now accept what before he rejected? The answer lies in his remoulding of kingship, about which he will be articulate in dialogue with Pilate a few days later.

My kingdom is not from this world. If my kingdom were from this world, my followers would be fighting to keep me from being handed over to the Jews. But as it is, my kingdom is not from here. (John 18.36)

Jesus is a profoundly original thinker. Every term of address that he receives is accepted, but reinterpreted, almost, you could say, turned on its head. 'You are the Messiah.' 'Yes, but if I am the Messiah, it is not the sort of messiah you envisage. Remember Caesarea Philippi.' 'You are the Christ, the Son of the living God.' 'Yes, but I must go to Jerusalem and suffer many things and be killed. Not your idea of a messiah, but a whole new interpretation.' It is the same with 'You are Master'. As he washes his disciples' feet, he redefines that role, the master who becomes the slave. 'You are the Son of man' is reinterpreted into a new vision of authentic humanity. And now 'You are a king'. Yes, but.

What sort of king is he who rides into the holy city? How is kingship moulded in his creative hands? First the king comes with humility, as Zechariah had said. He rides a beast of burden, a young ass rather than a war charger. Here is something new, a reinterpretation of kingship, with humility as its mark. Yet it is still as a leader that he rides into the city. He has not abdicated his responsibility. He will lead into battle. He will not hang back or surround himself with bodyguards, or send others in to be struck down first. Furthermore he will, if necessary, wage war single-handed. He will take on the enemy champion in combat and win. The king will die for his people without a thought to personal cost, and thus will blaze the trail into the freedom of the promised land for all his people. But the weapons are novel and the power a strange unpromising sort where strength seems to be weakness and human standards have no meaning. The cry *Hosanna* is henceforth to be for a new kind of leader, one who comes in gentleness, in simplicity and even in weakness.

We cannot know what thoughts and emotions were passing through the mind of Jesus as he rode into the city. He knew that his hour was coming and he understood at least in part what that must mean. He knew himself to be a king. He knew that the crown would be pressed upon him. But he knew that his kingdom was not of this world. Perhaps, being human, he responded with exhilaration and delight at the joyful festive reception that accompanied his arrival. But probably even then he knew the shallowness of human, worldly praise and hero-worship. Maybe he sat light to all the excitement and the fuss. Or maybe in the excitement of the crowd he perceived the return to test him again of that devil he had so summarily dismissed after his first anointing by the bank of the Jordan. 'When the devil had finished every test, he departed from him until an opportune time' (Luke 4.13).

In the centuries since and in the liturgy today what we are trying to do at the beginning of Holy Week is to get inside the mind of this Jesus who finally embraced the idea of kingship and yet transformed it. With the crowds in Jerusalem and with Christians the world over each Palm Sunday we find ourselves acclaiming:

> Blessed is the king, who comes in the name of the Lord! Peace in heaven, and glory in the highest heaven! (Luke 19.38)

Origins

Egeria in Jerusalem in the late fourth century experienced a Palm Sunday afternoon liturgy. At one o'clock they gathered for a service at the Eleona Church on the Mount of Olives lasting three hours, then moved to the Imbomon (the place where

Jesus is supposed to have ascended into heaven) for another service lasting till five o'clock. At the conclusion of that service Matthew's account of the entry into Jerusalem is read and then, Egeria continues,

> The bishop and all the people rise from their places, and start off on foot down from the summit of the Mount of Olives. All the people go before him with psalms and antiphons, all the time repeating: 'Blessed is he that cometh in the name of the Lord'. The babies and the ones too young to walk are carried on their parents' shoulders. Everyone is carrying branches, either of palm or olive, and they accompany the bishop in the very way the people did when once they went down with the Lord. They go on foot all down the Mount to the city, and all through the city to the Anastatis [the main church, of the resurrection], but they have to go pretty gently on account of the older women and men among them who might get tired.

Something like this can be seen developing in the liturgical life of the Church in the following centuries, inevitably the celebration becoming more complex and, to use Kenneth Stevenson's word, more 'representational'. Perhaps the most significant development was the move, with the tidying up of the liturgy, into the church building. Processions to the church turned into processions round the church interior and in time processions that people joined became processions by ministers with the people watching. At the Reformation in England this all disappeared. The entire palm liturgy was excised and even the name 'Palm Sunday' disappeared from 1549 in favour of 'The Sunday Next before Easter'. All that was left to make this day special was the reading of a longer than usual Gospel, Matthew's account of the Passion. It was the proposed Prayer Book of 1928 that reintroduced the name 'Palm Sunday', but was also responsible for an unfortunate development that made the Palm Gospel and the Passion Gospel alternatives (providing the Passion was read at one service), for it led in some communities to the celebration of the triumphal entry without taking the story forward to the events of later in the week. That has continued to be a regrettable element of Palm Sunday observance in some places.

Liturgy

However, before ever *Lent, Holy Week, Easter* was published churches were beginning to recover the idea of a participative procession often from outside the church building. *Lent, Holy Week, Easter* simply provided the text and some helpful guidance. The service in *Times and Seasons* (p. 269ff.) makes only very minimal changes. It assumes a liturgy that will start in one place and end in another. Depending on local circumstances it may be from one church to another; it may be from a village green or a school playing field, an open space some distance from the church; it might be from the church hall; it might be from the shopping centre or the supermarket car park (by arrangement!); it might be from the lychgate, if there is one and a shorter walk is necessary. It needs to be a sufficient distance from the church to allow for a significant movement from one place to another. It needs to be sufficiently close to the church that large numbers of people do not opt out and go straight to the church, missing the palm liturgy. It is always wise to bear in mind what Egeria wrote, 'they have to go pretty gently on account of the older women and men among them who might get tired'.

Times and Seasons says that 'palm or other branches may be used' and 'the congregation may bring palms with them or be given them as they arrive'. Palm trees are not, of course, to be found in the English countryside or indeed in the urban centres and we have noted already that only John speaks of palm, Mark of 'leafy branches'. Leafy branches of whatever tree seem to be a proper inculturation of the liturgy, whether palm, yew, forsythia or willow. Indeed willow has been called 'English palm'. It is important not to denude the countryside or the gardens, but it is not difficult with judicious pruning to find sufficient branches. In many ways that is more authentic than the dried palm branches that some churches store from year to year and bring out simply for this morning. It is also more authentic than commercially produced palm crosses, though they are a potent reminder of Holy Week for people to take home on Palm Sunday and retain through the week and maybe beyond it. There is every reason for people to hold up both a branch and a palm cross to be blessed at the appropriate moment in the service.

This outdoor liturgy may be as formal or as informal as the community decides. Where there is formality, with a robed choir and many ministers in robes and vestments, there will need to have been careful thought about how they are placed to create a worship space. One thing that should not happen is that they process formally together to the worship space. They need to arrive, however robed they are, informally, for the liturgy begins here, not in the church. But the gathering may be a much less formal one, with, people, armed with their branches, their palm crosses and a service sheet, crowding around a central point with a presiding minister and maybe a deacon and, if numbers are large, some means of amplification.

Ideally the liturgy begins with a sung hosanna. Texts are provided, but other hosanna songs would be appropriate. The president greets the people and introduces the service using the text provided or similar words, after which the people are invited to hold up their 'palms' for a prayer of blessing. They continue to hold them up as the palm Gospel is read – Matthew in Year A, Mark or John in Year B and Luke in Year C. After that the president invites everyone to 'go forth, praising Jesus our Messiah'.

The procession is not principally an act of witness. If it turns out to be this, well and good, but that is not the primary aim. It is a religious action to enrich the experience of the participant, not the onlooker, though if some onlookers turn into participants that is a bonus. It functions at two levels and sometimes they can feel like a tension. It recaptures something of the festivity and joy of the first Palm Sunday, with Christ the king entering his city. At the same time it is the beginning of the Holy Week walk that will continue right to the cross on Good Friday. This is well symbolized if the procession is led by a cross, perhaps a cross to which palms have been tied.

Because it is a joyful occasion, music and singing will be better than walking in silence. A band would help enormously or, at very least, any choir or set of singers, better placed in the middle of the procession rather than at the front. 'All glory, laud and honour' (*A&M* 159) is the traditional hymn for the procession. 'Make way, make way, for Christ the Lord' (*A&M* 160) and 'You are the King of glory' (*A&M* 164) are other possibilities from a different genre. 'Lift high the cross' (*A&M* 707), with its repeated refrain, is easy to sing even if it focuses more on the cross than on the triumphal entry. In *Ancient & Modern* Paul Wigmore has provided new Palm Sunday words to go with the 'Sing Hosanna' chorus, 'There's a man riding in on a donkey' (*A&M* 163). The reality is that, if the procession is drawn out (better to have a crowd than a crocodile!) people will get out of time with one another and generally there will be a degree of chaos. But that does not matter. The entry into Jerusalem does not seem to have been neat and tidy.

But what about the donkey? The tradition has had no place for one. *Times and Seasons* does not mention one. But they are a much loved feature of the day, especially in rural parishes. The reason for hesitation is that the donkey, complete with a ring of daffodils around its neck, becomes the dominant symbol, the focus, of the day and people come for or remember, not the walking with Christ or the hearing later of the passion, but the donkey. You have to ask where Jesus is to be found on this occasion, and he is not on a donkey and certainly not just in the child who might be placed upon the donkey, but among his people. He is present in his Church, hidden in the company of the faithful as they walk. So there is a reason for wariness about the donkey. On the other hand, as a draw, an evangelistic tool, the donkey is a winner, so it comes back to the question of whether this is 'rememorative' worship, as the liturgy usually is, or 'representational' worship which has more of a mission focus. I remember that, when I was a curate, we had the best of both worlds, a fairly formal procession to the church in the morning with no donkey and a lively informal pageant of a procession with a donkey through one of the estates of the parish in the afternoon, telling the story for those for whom this might be the closest they got to sharing in the parish's celebration of Holy Week.

Returning to the liturgical context, the procession reaches the church door. Here it is probably best to let everyone enter the church before the ministers. Ideally they throw down their branches in a pile outside the church. Some of them might later be burned in the new fire of Easter. Just a few of them might be stored to make ash for Lent next year. The important thing is that there should be a dramatic change of mood at this point. The liturgy of palms, the liturgy in the open air, is left behind, and the liturgy of the Passion, inside the church, takes its place. This is one of three moments in the liturgy of Holy Week where there is a sharp change that moves the story on. The choice of hymns, songs and anthems should reflect this and focus on the cross. The hymn 'Ride on, ride on, in majesty' (A&M 161) is particularly effective in changing the mood and is appropriately sung as the ministers enter the church. Hosannas are left outside along with the branches.

The service allows for rich provision of Scripture. There may be a reading from Isaiah (50.4-9a), eight verses of a psalm (31.9-16) and a reading from Philippians (2.5-11) and then the Passion. In many contexts this will, especially after the palm Gospel outside, be too much. The really important thing is that the Passion is read. For all their appropriateness the other readings and the psalm are there to enhance the Passion. A longer and a shorter form of it are given. The Passion varies, following the same three-year cycle as the rest of the year. (John is kept for Good Friday.) Sometimes, especially where there is a much loved musical setting of the Passion, there is a temptation to use that one every year. This needs to be resisted. It makes no sense in the year of Luke, for instance, suddenly to revert to Matthew on this one Sunday. The three-year cycle is probably more important on Palm Sunday than on any other day.

The Passion can be read by a single voice, as the Prayer Book envisaged, but it is a long passage to treat in this way. Traditionally it has three readers and a chorus. Musically, where the Passion is sung, the choir provides the chorus. In recent years there has been a move towards a more dramatic reading, with different people speaking all the different parts and the whole congregation becoming the chorus. Not only is this more dramatic, but it also identifies the congregation with those who called for Jesus to be crucified. That raises an issue. People will become more deeply involved if they are participating in this way. On the other hand there is a sense in which the people of God should have no part in crying out for the death of Jesus. They ought to listen silently aghast. Or, as can happen, they should speak, not the crowd texts, but the words of Jesus, seeking to identify with him in his passion. These are issues to be discussed locally. The decision in relation to the Passion on Palm Sunday does not necessarily need to be the same for John's Passion on Good Friday. The more the number of people involved in reading the Passion, the greater the need for rehearsal. It should be 'performed' in such a way that people are deeply moved.

There is no direction on posture for the Passion. Traditionally people have stood, as they do for the Gospel reading. But, if standing for a very long time leads them to be more concerned with keeping standing than focusing on the story, it would be better if they sat until the moment when Jesus is led out to be crucified, and remained standing then till the end.

The Passion read, there may be a brief sermon, though it is difficult to imagine that it should do more than encourage people to continue to walk with Christ through Holy Week and remind them of the opportunities to do so corporately in the coming days. Prayers of Intercession follow. The set text would not be improved by extempore interpolations. Then follows the Peace and thereafter the Eucharist continues along its usual lines, with a Preface of the Passion, with the words 'The body of Christ, broken for you' and 'The blood of Christ, shed for you' at the Distribution, with a special congregational Prayer after Communion and a Solemn Blessing. All these texts reinforce the basic message that we have left behind the palms and are walking with Jesus to the cross. People go home with that in their minds. It is unfortunate if they go home with the hosannas still ringing in their ears especially if they do not return until Easter with its alleluias.

We tend to assume the triumphal entry to be a morning event and to celebrate it in the morning, though we noted that Egeria and her companions celebrated it in the late afternoon. There is no reason why it should not be later in the day and in some churches in multi-parish benefices it is perhaps inevitable that it should be an afternoon celebration. What is important is that, once the liturgy has been celebrated, any further worship with the same community of people should not go back to the palms and reprise the hosannas. We have read the Passion and moved on. It is with clear intent that the New Testament reading set for Evening Prayer on Palm Sunday is always the parable of the wicked tenants:

> Finally he sent his son to them, saying, 'They will respect my son.' But when the tenants saw the son, they said to themselves, 'This is the heir; come, let us kill him and get his inheritance.' So they seized him, threw him out of the vineyard, and killed him. (Matthew 21.37-39)

6

Maundy Thursday

Triduum

Liturgists often speak of the period from the liturgy of Maundy Thursday evening until the end of the Easter liturgy as the *Triduum*. It simply means the 'Three Days'. The longer title is *Triduum Sacrum Paschale*, 'the Holy Paschal Three Days'. Originally it was taken to mean Good Friday, Easter Eve and Easter Day. Now it usually refers to three liturgies, the first on Maundy Thursday night, the second on Good Friday, the third to bring in the Easter season. Whether one uses the name *Triduum* or not, the important truth that it indicates is that we are dealing here with a unity, a continuum, not least because what is now celebrated in three separate liturgies was originally celebrated in one on Easter night.

Scripture

It would be too easy to think of Maundy Thursday as simply about the institution of the Eucharist. The liturgy has to capture a whole series of words and incidents spread through the day and the evening. Matthew (26.17–56) and Mark (14.12–52) recount the events of this day almost identically, though some of the fascination is in the variations in Luke (22.7–62). They all speak of the 'first day of unleavened bread' and tell of the preparations for the supper, which is to be a Passover meal, and of the meal itself in which Jesus commands his friends to eat bread, his body, and drink wine, the blood of the covenant.

Luke, like Paul in 1 Corinthians (11.24), has Jesus say, 'Do this in remembrance of me.' He also has a more complex account of the supper, with two separate cups and the giving of the bread between the sharing of the cups. They all have Jesus add that he will never again drink of the fruit of the vine 'until that day that I drink it new with you in my Father's kingdom'.

Luke also interpolates at the supper a dispute about which of the disciples is to be regarded as the greatest. 'For who is greater,' Jesus asks,

> the one who is at the table or the one who serves? Is it not the one at the table? But I am among you as one who serves. (Luke 22.27)

There are echoes here of the story that John will tell of the washing of the disciples' feet at the meal. Luke also places the prediction of Peter's denial within the supper:

> I tell you, Peter, the cock will not crow this day, until you have denied three times that you know me. (Luke 22.34)

They sing a hymn and then go out to the Mount of Olives and it is there that Matthew and Mark have Peter's denial predicted. Matthew and Mark recount the events on the Mount of Olives in almost identical words. Jesus goes to Gethsemane, taking Peter, James and John. He is grieved and agitated, leaves the three, bidding them 'stay awake with him', and goes on to be in a place alone, where he prays to his Father that, if it is possible, the cup 'might pass him by'. 'Yet, not what I want, but what you want' (Mark 14.36). He comes back, finds the three sleeping, urges them to stay awake and pray that they may not come to the time of trial, and returns to his prayer, asking the same question, but again with an acceptance of his vocation. He comes to the three a third time and finds them sleeping again, and now it is time for the drama to move on. 'My betrayer is at hand' (Mark 14.42).

Luke handles this stage in the evening a little differently. There is no mention of Gethsemane, nor are three disciples singled out. Instead, there on the Mount of Olives all the disciples are urged to pray that they may not come to the time of trial. Jesus, a stone's throw away, prays just once his prayer of acceptance of the Father's will. A disputed verse not found in all early manuscripts says:

> Then an angel from heaven appeared to him and gave him strength. In his anguish he prayed more earnestly, and his sweat became like great drops of blood falling down on the ground. (Luke 22.43f.)

When he returns to the disciples they are sleeping 'because of grief'. But they must get up for the crowd, with Judas in its midst, is approaching.

Matthew, Mark and Luke are very close to one another in what follows. Judas arrives with a large crowd from the priests and elders, soldiers among them, Judas intending to betray Jesus with a kiss. There is a scuffle, the high priest's servant loses an ear, although in Luke Jesus heals him. Jesus asks why they have come out to arrest him as if he were a bandit, but he knows it is all taking place 'so that the scriptures of the prophets may be fulfilled. This is your hour and the power of darkness!' (Matthew 26.56; Luke 22.53) 'Then all the disciples deserted him and fled,' Matthew tells us (26.56f.); and Mark adds:

> A certain young man was following him, wearing nothing but a linen cloth. They caught hold of him, but he left the linen cloth and ran off naked. (Mark 14.51f.)

The scene moves to the house of the high priest, or more precisely to its courtyard where there is a fire burning. Three times Simon Peter is asked whether he is a disciple of Jesus, for even his accent gives him away, but three times Peter denies it. It is only Luke who tells us that Jesus turned and looked at Peter, but all three record that, when the cock crew, Peter remembered what Jesus had said and went out and wept bitterly.

Very different is the Fourth Gospel's account of the same day. John also has a Maundy Thursday supper, though in his chronology it is not the Passover meal. He does not give us the words about the bread as the body of Christ or the wine as his blood. He does not include the command to 'do this in remembrance of me', but there is a supper nevertheless. He tells us that during supper Jesus gets up from the table (13.4), that one of the disciples was reclining next to Jesus (13.25) and that Jesus dipped a piece of bread in the dish before giving it to Judas (13.26f.). The meal was the context for an action of profound significance, for a wealth of teaching, for the foretelling of both a betrayal and a denial, for the urging of a new commandment and for the offering of a prayer. It all happens at the meal table and John fills four chapters (12–17) in the telling of it. The wealth of teaching, which the Fourth Gospel places on the lips of Jesus as he sits there at the table, is about himself as the Way, the Truth and the Life and as the Vine, about the promise of the Spirit and about his return to the Father. His invitation to them to love one another, his new commandment is, ironically, sandwiched between his foretelling of the betrayal by Judas and of the denial of Peter. But then he turns his attention away from his disciples, though, as the evangelist records it, they are still in the room, as he prays to his Father, the 'high-priestly prayer' as it has been called, praying that they, and those who come after, may be one, as he and the Father are one. It is on that note of prayer, focused on the Father, that he leads them out across the Kidron valley to the garden where he will be arrested, though for him there is no agony in that garden. Instead he asks with utter confidence, 'Am I not to drink the cup that the Father has given me?' (John 18.11).

But that is to jump ahead. Before that comes the action of profound significance. It is, of course, the washing of the disciples' feet by Jesus. It was just before the festival of the Passover. Jesus knew that his hour to depart had come. He

> got up from the table, took off his outer robe, and tied a towel around himself. Then he poured water into a basin and began to wash the disciples' feet and to wipe them with the towel that was tied around him. He came to Simon Peter, who said to him, 'Lord, are you going to wash my feet?' Jesus answered, 'You do not know now what I am doing, but later you will understand.' (John 13.4–7)

Peter is reluctant at first, but when he begins to understand asks that Jesus will wash not only his feet, but also his hands and his head. The language of washing, bathing and cleansing is reminiscent of baptism. Once again robed and sitting at the table Jesus gives a new commandment to wash one another's feet and goes on to spell out something more fundamental, a foundational new commandment, that they love one another. Just as he has loved them, they are to love one another. That is the new commandment, *mandatum*, that gives this Thursday of Holy Week its name – Maundy, *Mandatum*, Thursday, New Commandment Thursday.

Washing feet

What does this stupendous, yet strangely homely and intimate sacramental moment mean? It means, first of all, something about humility. The humility of Jesus lies in the truth of who he really is. It is not the humility of a man that is demonstrated in this story, but the nature of God that is revealed. Here is a reminder, as we enter the passion, of the truth that Christmas first spelt out. The great God, the creator of heaven and earth, has taken on human shape and form and nature, as a weak and helpless baby. The one who rules the constellations has made a home in a human body. Too easily we call that 'incarnation' and by giving it a name make manageable an almost incomprehensible truth. The very thought of it should bring us to our knees, as it did shepherds and magi alerted by angels and star. But here we discover, when the child has grown into a man, not that we are brought to our knees by this tremendous mystery, but that it is he, this God in Christ, who falls to his knees to wash the feet and wipe them with the towel.

The action also speaks of service. Although it is only John who tells this story, we have already noted how Luke has spoken about the one who serves at table; and earlier in the Gospel story Mark has Jesus say:

> You know that among the Gentiles those whom they recognize as their rulers lord it over them, and their great ones are tyrants over them. But it is not so among you; but whoever wishes to be great among you must be your servant, and whoever wishes to be first among you must be slave of all. For the Son of Man came not to be served but to serve, and to give his life a ransom for many. (Mark 10.42–45)

It is another stage in Jesus' revolution, his turning on its head of much conventional wisdom. Henceforth the mark of authority is to be service. The greatest in the kingdom will be the ones who are willing to serve brothers and sisters in the most menial of stations.

But, for all the richness of their meaning within the context of this story, both these words – humility and service – seem inadequate to express what Jesus is doing and bids us do. Only a third word expresses strongly enough what is at stake. For Jesus does not talk about humility, nor in John about service, but about love.

> I give you a new commandment, that you love one another, just as I have loved you. (John 13.34)

For good measure he adds that it is by this love for one another that everyone will know we are his disciples. It is only love that expresses strongly enough what is being shown here.

For it is love that best describes what Jesus does when he fetches bowl and water, jug and towel. It is not simply the humility of the God who is on his knees, nor the lesson in service of the master who behaves like a slave, but the love of one who is generous, warm, impulsive and affectionate in his loving. Jesus is not giving an object lesson in good relationships. Nor is he acting out a sort of parable. He is doing it because he wants to do it. He is doing it because the tired, hot, sweaty feet in need of washing are the feet that belong to his friends, his close companions, his adopted family. It is an act of love, generous, embarrassing, natural love. We must not imagine for a moment a solemn ecclesiastical ritual. This is a joyful act of self-giving. And Jesus adds, to hammer home the point,

By this everyone will know that you are my disciples, if you have love for one another. (John 13.35)

People will know that there is something of Christ in you if there is a warmth, a joy, a natural affection, an impulsive generosity breaking out in all your human relationships. That understanding of what is going on when Jesus washes feet needs to shape how we make the footwashing our own in the liturgy of Maundy Thursday.

This account of the story of Maundy Thursday makes it obvious that, to do justice to the day, there has to be an engagement with more than one mood and more than one event. The truth is that some Christians will miss out on all of this, the ones who go straight from Palm Sunday to Good Friday or even from Palm Sunday to Easter Day. It is also true that Christians who simply gather for an *agape* or a Eucharist much like the celebration on any other day will miss much of the rich subtlety of the day. Rather like Palm Sunday, with its move from palm to Passion, Maundy Thursday has to be a day where, within one liturgical event, people may move from the commemoration of the Last Supper, with its washing of feet and its joyful festivity in the institution of the Eucharist, into the very different experience of the Mount of Olives, the betrayal, the arrest and the denial. Although it has long been a principle to celebrate only one Eucharist on Maundy Thursday and that (at least for the last 60 years) in the evening, pastoral considerations may mean a second celebration for those unable to be present in the evening – older people who do not go out at night, or single parents with young children, for instance. Something of the special character of today can be retained if this is in the late afternoon rather than in the morning, especially as the clergy may be otherwise engaged in the morning by attending a great service in the cathedral.

Liturgy

In most dioceses there is on Maundy Thursday (in a few it is earlier in the week) what is often called the Chrism Mass, a Eucharist for the blessing of the holy oils and the renewal of ordination vows. Being a diocesan service, rather than one for each church community, it falls outside the compass of this book. Historically it began as a service to bless the oils in order that they could be used for baptism at Easter. Pope Paul VI added for Roman Catholics a renewal of ordination vows at that same service and most Anglican dioceses in England have followed suit. In many places it is now a very significant moment in the annual cycle of a diocese, with the great majority of the clergy gathered with their bishop, often with many lay people too. Maundy Thursday is thought by some to be a difficult date for clergy and others to make the journey to their cathedral (especially in geographically large rural dioceses) and another date has sometimes to be chosen, but clearly there is something very good about clergy being entirely on the receiving end of ministry just before they need to give so much in the leading of their congregations through the *Triduum*.

Times and Seasons provides a full Liturgy of Maundy Thursday. It is a liturgy of the upper room and of the garden of Gethsemane, not one or the other, but both. It does not provide for an *agape* on this day and that is wise, partly because an *agape* focuses exclusively on just one of the themes of the day, that of the fellowship of the supper to the inevitable neglect of other themes, but also because the Maundy Thursday liturgy needs to be sufficiently like what happens week by week for the connection to be made between this holy night and every celebration, though sufficiently different to allow the distinctive elements of this night to come into prominence. White is the liturgical colour, for this is not the purple or unbleached linen of Lent or the red of the Passion; but, if possible, nor is it the best white or gold of Easter.

There are a number of new hymns to enhance the Maundy Thursday liturgy, Among them are Fred Pratt Green's 'An upper room did our Lord prepare' (*A&M* 165), Brian Wren's 'Great God, your love has called us here' (*A&M* 169) and, best of all, Richard Sturch's translation of Peter Abélard's 'This is the night' (*A&M* 173), which sets the mood for the Eucharist wonderfully. If Hubert Parry's fine tune is unknown, the hymn also works well with J. B. Dykes' 'Strength and Stay' (*A&M* 21). Those unfamiliar with these hymns will find they are a fine resource for this service. But some of the traditional eucharistic hymns also have their place. James Montgomery's 'According to thy gracious word' (*A&M* 420) is particularly apt, with its repeated 'I will remember thee'.

The service begins with the Greeting in the 'grace of our Lord Jesus Christ' form, with its emphasis on love and fellowship, and will almost everywhere need to be followed by a short informal introduction by the president. At this point there is the possibility of receiving into the church the community's share of the holy oils blessed earlier by the bishop in the cathedral. *Times and Seasons* provides a short text for this (p. 292), though there is an extraordinary error that allocates texts to the 'bishop' rather than the 'president'. This text and ceremony need add very little time to the service, but link the community with the diocese and the bishop in a meaningful way and, if there are to be baptisms in Eastertide, make a helpful link.

The Prayers of Penitence follow, with special texts appropriate to the day, leading into the Gloria. Traditionally the Gloria, which has been silent through Lent, returns, because, for all the solemnity, this is a joyful celebration. There is a long tradition of all singing being unaccompanied after this Gloria until Easter and where there are strong and confident voices to lead the singing it adds to the uniqueness of the *Triduum*, but not every community could maintain that.

After the Gloria, the invitation to pray and the Collect follow. The readings are the same in all three years – the instructions relating to the Passover meal from Exodus, Paul's account of the Last Supper from 1 Corinthians, together with psalm and Gospel acclamation, all leading to the Gospel reading, which recounts the footwashing.

There are clearly two ways of approaching the footwashing. It is possible to combine it with the Gospel reading, pausing part way through the Gospel for the action of washing feet and then, when that is complete, reading the remainder of the Gospel reading. Or it is possible (and *Times and Seasons* goes with this option) to read the Gospel in the normal way, move on to the sermon and then have the footwashing after the sermon.

The washing of feet is gradually re-establishing itself in Anglican practice, but there has been reluctance and it is not difficult to know the reason. This is not a tidy ritual, nor one that can be made wholly elegant. Water, feet and priests on their knees with bowls and towels does not fit easily into most people's idea of Anglican ceremonial, and the more solemn you try to make it to compensate, the more farcical it could become. But those who have taken the plunge, so to speak, would nearly all urge on their fellow Christians that they do include this in their liturgy on Maundy Thursday. Ritual is nearly always more fruitful for those who participate in it than for those who merely observe it. Each year priests are given a marvellously humbling, yet uplifting experience, as they kneel to minister to members of their community, and each year 12 different people in the community are given the experience, as marvellously humbling, yet uplifting, of receiving this ministry. It is worth it for what it does for 13 people each year, however little it may do for the observers, though they do very often catch the atmosphere too. And if it is not tidy and elegant, perhaps there is a lesson to be learned in that too!

I say '12', as 12 has been the tradition on this day. John's account speaks of the 'disciples' and people have imagined the 12 apostles. But there is an argument for more or fewer people depending on local circumstances. Certainly the Roman provision for it to be 12 men is unfortunate, and if the gender is not important, nor is the number. I say 'priests', but there is nothing narrowly priestly about exercising this ministry. In some communities there has been a more free and easy approach where several people wash feet and where those who wash feet also have their feet washed by others. There is no one right way, but it is worth bearing in mind that, as Jesus modelled this sacramental act, he did it as 'teacher and lord'. It was the action of the master being the servant. We should be careful in appearing to identify master and servant with priest and parishioners, but there is a sense in which this is about the stripping away of authority and an appropriateness about the person who presides in the community exercising this ministry. If they do so, they do not so much exercise their priesthood as their diaconate.

Who should receive this ministry of footwashing? In some communities it is left to those who volunteer, maybe just those who come forward or take off their shoes on the night. That, of course, does not address the kind of reluctance that Simon Peter showed. Often it is those who are least likely to volunteer who might be most helped or healed by the experience. Even when things are left open for people to 'opt in', it would be wise for some people to have been chosen and briefed beforehand, and not immediately beforehand, so that they can have thought about what to be wearing. There should be some attempt at gender parity and some attempt to have a wide age range. I have always thought it helpful to think of people for whom this is a special time in their life – a candidate for baptism or confirmation, a person recently bereaved, a couple soon to be married, a young person about to go away to college, a person with a sense of vocation developing. In my experience, if Holy Week is a time when people's lives can be transformed, this is one of the moments when this can be happen. It can have a profound effect and be a moment of inspiration, conversion, reconciliation or healing. Not to be offering it is a missed opportunity and a shame.

This is a down-on-the-floor ministry. Those whose feet are to be washed should not be seated on a platform or up a set of steps. Whether they move to seats in an open space or whether they sit on the end of rows of seating so that the ministers may reach them, this is essentially a down-on-the-floor moment, whatever the loss of visual impact for others.

It is important that this washing of feet should not be hurried and, especially as the congregation cannot all be visually engaged all the time, there needs to be good music to accompany the footwashing. The traditional song for this moment is *Ubi caritas* – 'God is love, and where true love is, God himself is there'. It was especially composed for the footwashing in a Benedictine community in Reichenau around the beginning of the ninth century. The version printed in *Times and Seasons* (p. 298) is by James Quinn and the music is to be found in many contemporary hymn and song books (*A&M* 168). In places where there are suitable musical resources there is Maurice Duruflé's setting of the Latin text. More simply, there is the Taizé setting of the key line – *Ubi caritas et amor, deus ibi est.* I am unsure why Geoffrey Preston's loose translation, which can be sung to any common metre tune, has not appeared in the most recent hymn books. It is worth recovering.

Where love and loving-kindness dwell,
there God will ever be:
One Father, Son, and Holy Ghost
in perfect charity.

Brought together into one
by Christ our shepherd-king,
now let us in his love rejoice,
and of his goodness sing.

Here too let God, the living God,
both loved and honoured be;
and let us each the other love
with true sincerity.

Brought here together by Christ's love,
let no ill-will divide,
nor quarrels break the unity
of those for whom he died.

Let envy, jealousy and strife
and all contention cease,
for in our midst serves Christ the Lord,
our sacrament of peace.

Together may we with the saints
thy face in glory see,
and ever in thy kingdom feast,
O Christ our God, with thee.

But there are other songs – 'A new commandment I give unto you' and 'Let there be love shared among us' in *Hymns Old and New* 34 and 134, and 'Faith, hope and love, these three shall remain' in *Ancient & Modern* 167. For churches with choirs there is also Thomas Tallis' 'If ye love me'.

Jesus 'laid aside his garments'. Where the tradition is for the president to wear a chasuble, he or she might well 'lay it aside' at this point in the service. A priest might adjust the stole to wear it over the left shoulder as a deacon to exercise a diaconal ministry. The president goes in turn to each person whose feet are to be washed. There is a need for a second minister, since there are bowl, jug and towels to be carried, but as far as possible this is a ministry best done without attendants. Jesus is not described as having others to assist him! Each footwashing must come over as a warm and human action of affection and service, not as a rather clinical liturgical ceremony. It needs to be a proper washing of both feet, pouring water into the bowl over the feet, and a proper drying of them too. The president may well speak a brief word with each person. In some traditions the president kisses the feet that have been washed. Others may prefer a clasping of the hand, rather than a kissing of the foot, before moving to the next person. When the president has completed the footwashing there is a Collect to conclude this stage in the liturgy before the Prayers of Intercession, which are particular to Maundy Thursday.

After the exchange of the Peace comes the Preparation of the Gifts with the singing of a hymn. How much bread and wine is brought to the altar table depends on the intention in relation to Holy Communion on Good Friday. The case for this will be discussed in Chapter 7, but, if there is to be Holy Communion on Good Friday from pre-sanctified elements (i.e. bread and wine consecrated on Maundy Thursday and used next day), there will need to be sufficient bread consecrated for both days and, if people are to receive in both kinds, an additional flagon of wine.

Even in communities where the liturgy usually moves straight from a hymn into the Eucharistic Prayer, there is a case on Maundy Thursday for special material at this point. The texts provided bring out the Passover origins of the Eucharist and, to an extent, employ words Jesus may himself have used if there was indeed a Passover meal.

The Eucharistic Prayer follows, with a Preface unique to this day. A note, easily missed, also invites the president, in saying the Eucharistic Prayer, to insert, after the words 'in the same night that he was betrayed' or the equivalent words, the phrase 'that is, this very night', though that is a clumsy adaptation and it would be better to substitute 'in this very night when he was betrayed'. Among the *Common Worship* options the words at the Breaking of the Bread, at the Invitation to Communion and during the Distribution that underline the passion are to be preferred, especially 'The body of Christ, broken for you' and 'The blood of Christ, shed for you'. The Post Communion Prayer is Thomas Aquinas' great eucharistic collect and it rounds off this part of the service and brings us to a moment of transition.

Watch

At this point there are important decisions to be made. Is there to be a Watch, responding to Jesus' request to his followers on the Mount of Olives to 'watch and pray'? If there is a Watch, who will keep watch? If there is to be a Watch, where is it to be and how will the space be furnished? Will it be in the presence of the Blessed Sacrament and how is the Sacrament to be brought to this space? Are the altar and sanctuary to be stripped bare? If there is a Watch, will it be silent or will there be readings and prayers? How and when will it end? The appropriate answer to the later questions will vary from one community to another. But the answer to the first question – Is there to be a Watch? – ought nearly always to be yes. Without it there is the danger that people will go home carrying only the memory of the footwashing, the meal and the joyful intimacy. It is crucial that they experience the mood change of going out 'into the night', so to speak, sharing, as far as they are able, the Gethsemane experience and following Jesus through the betrayal, the arrest and the denial before he comes to his time of trial. *Times and Seasons* does provide a short ending, with just a hint of the Watch.

> When the disciples had sung a hymn they went out to the Mount of Olives. Jesus prayed to the Father, 'If it is possible, take this cup of suffering from me.' He said to his disciples, 'How is it that you were not able to keep watch with me for one hour? The hour has come for the Son of Man to be handed over to the power of sinners.' Christ was obedient unto death. Go in his peace. (p. 304)

This is intentionally austere. There is no Blessing and no response to the Dismissal. But it is a poor substitute for a Watch. If we leave without the Watch, the words of Jesus would be ringing in our ears, 'How is it that you were not able to keep watch for one hour?'

So, on the assumption of a Watch, we need to address the subsequent questions.

First, if there is to be a watch, who will keep watch? In many places where the Watch is to go on for several hours there will be a rota where people will have signed up for an hour or half an hour so that there are always some people present to watch and pray. That does not, of course, stop some people who are not on the rota from coming to share in it, nor does it make it wrong for some people to stay for the entirety of the Watch. But it is probably reassuring to know that someone will be there at every stage so the chain of prayer is not broken. Alternatively there is the possibility of a much shorter but communal Watch. For just an hour, or just half an hour, the whole community stays at prayer and the Watch is concluded at the end of their shared vigil of prayer.

Second, where is the Watch to be and how will the space be furnished? Although it is possible to make the whole church the space for the Watch and the main altar the focus, the tradition has been to focus the Watch in a smaller and more intimate space, classically a side chapel or around an altar set up in a different part of the building. In the more catholic tradition, with the Blessed Sacrament as the focus, an altar, referred to as 'the altar of repose', has been surrounded by lighted candles and flowers. An alternative is to place plants and flowers at points around the floor, creating a kind of Gethsemane Garden, rather than all the flowers in one place. There needs to be space for people to kneel. There also need to be chairs, stools or benches around the edge of the space so that people may sit. There needs to be a little restrained lighting, especially if people are to be able to read. The rest of the church may be mostly in darkness once the liturgy of the Last Supper is over, but the arrangements should allow for any who so wish to keep watch in the shadows of the main church rather than in the intimacy of the designated space. Within that space there does need to be a focus. If the Blessed Sacrament on the altar is not to be that focus, another needs to be created.

Third, will the Watch be in the presence of the Blessed Sacrament? There are clearly two clear arguments, aside from tradition, in favour. One is partially a practical one. If there is to be Holy Communion on Good Friday (and in Chapter 7 I will argue strongly for that), then consecrated bread and possibly wine need to be kept, 'reserved', from the Maundy Thursday Eucharist for use next day. As such a ciborium or other container of consecrated bread and a flagon of consecrated wine placed upon the 'altar of repose' and honoured with candles is a natural and practical arrangement. But there are churches that do not have Holy Communion on Good Friday that nevertheless keep Watch before the Blessed Sacrament, even if the consecrated elements are consumed when the Watch ends. This is, of course, because the sacramental presence of Christ enhances for those who share in the Watch the sense of being with Christ, keeping watch with him in an intimate way. Nothing else, not even an icon or a cross (better kept for Good Friday) or the Book of the Gospels, serves so effectively as the sacramental presence through these hours.

Fourth, how is the Blessed Sacrament to be brought to this Gethsemane space? Again there is a catholic tradition or something more simple. The catholic tradition involves a procession after the Post Communion Prayer from the altar of celebration to the altar of repose, certainly with candles, possibly with incense, bringing the Sacrament to its new setting. It may be something the whole community watches from afar. On the other hand it may be a procession in which they join, staying then, for a while at least, to begin the Watch. The hymn that usually accompanies such a procession is Thomas Aquinas' great eucharistic song, 'Now, my tongue, the mystery telling' (*A&M* 457), with the final two verses – 'Therefore we before

him bending this great sacrament revere . . .' – being sung
kneeling before the sacrament on the altar of repose. But the
sacrament could be conveyed to its new setting without such
ceremony and without singing. As a transition from the meal to
the garden, John Henry Newman's hymn, 'Praise to the holiest
in the height' (A&M 763), is extraordinarily effective, especially with the omission of the final verse so that it ends:

And in the garden secretly,
and on the cross on high,
should teach his brethren,
and inspire to suffer and to die.

Fifth, are the altar and sanctuary to be stripped bare? The purpose of this is partly practical, a desire that the church shall be
as austere and bereft of light and colour as possible for Good
Friday, in contrast to what will happen at Easter. But there
is also a sense in which the stripping seems to represent the
stripping of Christ in preparation for crucifixion. This stripping can be done quite informally when the people have gone,
whether in silence or with some texts, and if the focus has
already moved to the Watch that may be best. But there is the
possibility, once the Blessed Sacrament has been moved, of the
stripping bare of altar and sanctuary to be done in full view
of the congregation. The style can vary. In some places a care-
fully rehearsed ceremony, executed by robed ministers, as the
lights are gradually put down, with appropriate texts, moves
the mood from joyful supper to fearful garden. The candles are
extinguished, the vessels and other material from the Eucharist
removed, the coverings of the altar taken off and carried away,
the movable furnishings apart from the altar also, so that the
sanctuary is left stark and bare.

In other places there is a preference for a rather frenzied
stripping bare, with people rushing hither and thither with the
artefacts they remove, reminiscent of the fleeing of the disciples
from the garden. It is an uncomfortable end.

Sung texts add to the effectiveness of the stripping. Traditionally Psalm 22 has been used (though that will occur again on Good Friday). Psalm 69.1–22 is also suitable. *Times and Seasons* has a sequence of verses from Lamentations (p. 303). For those with the musical resources there is a fine setting by Sir Edward Bairstow. Spoken texts are probably less effective and silence may be preferred. Whether words, singing or silence the aim is to heighten the moment of transition 'into the night'.

Sixth, returning to the Watch, will it be silent or will there be readings and prayers? The tradition is silence, but not all communities will find that helpful. *Times and Seasons* provides a sequence of readings from chapters 13 to 17 of John's Gospel, with a portion of the *Hallel* psalms of the Passover (113 to 118) after each (p. 304). These will only be appropriate during a long watch of several hours, for the words should never do more than stimulate the silence into reflection and prayer. If there is a need for quiet singing, the repeated use of the Taizé chant, 'Stay with me, remain here with me, watch and pray' (*A&M* 172) is appropriate.

Finally, how and when will the Watch end? There has been a tradition of the Watch continuing right through the night. In present Roman Catholic practice it continues until midnight. It has to be a pastoral judgement whether to continue till midnight or to finish earlier. *Times and Seasons* provides a Gospel of the Watch (p. 304) to be read at the conclusion, recounting all that happens after the supper until Jesus is brought to trial. The person reading it might add the words provided for places where there is no Watch.

Christ was obedient unto death. Go in his peace.

At whatever time in the evening people return to their homes, the aim has been to create within them a sense of watching and walking with Jesus through these hours. They will eventually go to sleep, but when they wake in the morning their thoughts will still be with Jesus and their participation in his passion real.

7

Good Friday

Origins

All four Gospel writers tell in more detail than any other event the story of Good Friday. It begins with the appearance before the Jewish Council leading into the trial before Pilate, in Luke's account something not unlike a second trial before King Herod, then the sentence to death, the mocking and scourging by the soldiers, and the journey, carrying the cross and falling under its weight, to Golgotha, the 'Place of the Skull'. There Jesus is crucified between two thieves and, after words of deep significance (varying from Gospel to Gospel), dies at three o'clock in the afternoon. Later his body is taken down and disciples bury him in a tomb. Other than 'the disciple whom Jesus loved' the apostles are nowhere to be seen. It is the women who stay the course.

Egeria gives us a fascinating account of Good Friday in fourth-century Jerusalem. It made serious demands on her and on all the participants, who did not, unlike even the most devout Christians today, have the opportunity to retire to bed at midnight. Instead there was a series of processional services in the early hours of Friday morning, which ended in a walk into the city to the main church, at the point where the crucifixion was believed to have taken place, Golgotha. Here the account of the trial before Pilate was read (John 18.28—19.16). The bishop then sent people home for some sleep, since, as Egeria notes, 'they have been hard at it all night, and there is further effort in store for them in the day ahead'.

The congregation reassembled at eight o'clock in the morning, when the 'holy wood of the cross' (the relic of the true cross as people believed) occupied the central place in a special and solemn liturgy. Egeria continued:

> The bishop's chair is placed on Golgotha . . . A table is placed before him with a cloth on it, the deacons stand round, and there is brought to him a gold and silver box containing the holy Wood of the Cross. It is opened, and the Wood of the Cross and the Title are taken out and placed on the table.
>
> As long as the holy Wood is on the table, the bishop sits with his hands resting on either end of it and holds it down, and the deacons round him keep watch over it. They guard it like this because what happens now is that all the people, catechumens as well as faithful, come up one by one to the table. They stoop down over it, kiss the Wood, and move on. But on one occasion (I don't know when) one of them bit off a piece of the holy Wood and stole it away, and for this reason the deacons stand round and keep watch in case anyone dares to do the same again. Thus all the people go past one by one. They stoop down, touch the holy Wood first with their forehead and then with their eyes, and then kiss it, but no one puts out his hand to touch it.

This ceremony went on until midday, which means it lasted a few hours. When it was over, there was a long service lasting three hours, which was made up of readings, psalms, epistles and Gospels, all concerned with the sufferings of Christ. Egeria hints that one of the Old Testament readings was the 'suffering servant' passage of Isaiah 52 and 53. She is clearly struck by the intense atmosphere. At three o'clock, the account of the death of Jesus was read, probably John 19.17–37. The day ended with a service which commemorated the burial of Christ celebrated at the tomb.

Changing patterns

That was Good Friday in fourth-century Jerusalem. There may be lessons we can learn from it for twenty-first-century Britain, urban or rural, for certainly we want people to be struck, and indeed changed, by the intense atmosphere. But Christian celebration has to respond to the way that Good Friday has changed in secular culture. Good Friday has never been a straightforward bank holiday of the old kind, with all places of work closed down and shops shut. In the Midlands and the north of England, at least, industry has never entirely stopped for Good Friday; but until a generation ago most shops were shut, the majority of people did not go to work, and the media, especially through television programmes, including acts of worship, highlighted that this was the day Jesus died. More people went to church than on an average Sunday. Today probably rather fewer people go to work on Good Friday, many have set off on holiday or to visit family over a four-day break, the shops are nearly all open, the media hardly draw attention to the fact that for Christians it is a special day, and the number of people taking part in Christian worship probably does not exceed the number on an ordinary Sunday. In some benefices some churches will have no service at all.

Clearly the secular cultural changes account for much of this, but we do need to ask whether they are entirely responsible for the decline in church attendance on Good Friday. Is the decline partly because of what the Church is offering on this day? Or is it because it is offering it at the wrong time? Or is it that the need to witness has eclipsed the need to worship? Most importantly, is the decline reversible? I believe it is.

We need to look first at the inherited pattern of Good Friday worship. In most church communities 50 years ago, there were probably three services, or maybe four.

The first, celebrated quite early in the day and attended by very few, was what the Book of Common Prayer seemed to order – 'Ante Communion', sometimes preceded by Morning

Prayer and the Litany. Ante Communion was the Eucharist cut short after the Prayers of Intercession because it was thought wrong to receive Communion on this day (about which more a little later). Within Ante Communion was the reading of John chapter 19, the second part of John's account of the Passion, the key biblical passage of the day, but heard in most places by a very small congregation. In just a few churches there was a more elaborate liturgy, based on Roman practice, that included 'the veneration of the cross' and, in even fewer places, the receiving of Holy Communion from the pre-sanctified elements.

The second service was one lasting from noon until three o'clock, referred to very often simply as 'the Three Hours'. Its origins, surprisingly, were Jesuit and Peruvian, but it had taken root in the Church of England. It consisted of a series of addresses by a single preacher, usually robed only in a black cassock, who never left the pulpit, often seven addresses based on the seven words Jesus spoke from the cross, together with hymns, prayers and silences. Some people stayed for all three hours. Most came for an hour and slipped in or out under cover of a hymn. As this form of worship, which depended so much on the skill of the preacher, declined, so that today it is found only in cathedrals and some major churches, a service of three hours tended to give way to a single hour, the hour leading up to the death of Jesus at three o'clock. It was thus right in the middle of the day. Its form was often a short version of the old preaching Three Hours. In the few places where 'the Three Hours' has remained it does often attract growing congregations of people looking for something substantial on Good Friday.

The third, at least in an urban setting, was an ecumenical gathering, very often outdoors, sometimes walking the way of the cross in silence, with 'stations' as a procession moved from one church to another, sometimes timed to catch shoppers and to make sure they were aware it was Good Friday, perhaps ending with a short service in one of the churches. The Passion story was almost certainly told, but in snippets at the stations along the way. Sometimes the procession would be headed by a group of men dragging a heavy wooden cross. A gathering like this would often have been in the early evening, but more often recently in the morning. This form of worship and witness can still be effective, though in general numbers taking part have declined and the impression made on the shoppers can be that here is a group of rather unhappy looking 'kill-joys' protesting against shopping on Good Friday, rather than Christians celebrating the victory of Jesus, lifted up on the cross, drawing all humanity to himself.

The fourth was a service for children, often mid-morning, trying to engage younger people with the mystery of the cross in an appropriate way, which was and is quite a challenge.

I have described this pattern in the past tense, but in many communities some of this remains and there has been no fundamental rethinking of Good Friday worship. The Ante Communion has almost certainly disappeared; the Three Hours has been reduced to one hour, and that hour tries to meet the spiritual needs of adults while also trying to engage children; and the ecumenical walk is probably less supported than in the past. Yet this is the day on which Jesus died for the sins of the world. This is the day when you would expect the liturgy to be at its most profound, most challenging and most transforming. As in Egeria's day, the hope must be that people are struck and changed by the atmosphere. What can be done?

The answer lies partly in thinking afresh about service times, partly in reflecting on how children may be catered for, partly in recognizing the need for both worship and witness, but mainly in discovering or rediscovering a liturgy that has the power to lead us deeply into the mystery of Christ's death. I say 'rediscovering' because much of what we need to create a compelling liturgy is to be found in fourth-century Jerusalem and developments from it, but 'discovering', perhaps for the first time, because there has been just such a liturgy available in the Church of England for more than 30 years, first in *Lent*,

Holy Week, Easter and later in *Times and Seasons*, but people do not seem to have discovered it in the way they have the liturgies of Palm Sunday, Maundy Thursday and Easter. It is not too late to find it.

Fourth Gospel

Before turning to the detail of that liturgy, it is worth pausing to establish the primacy of the Fourth Gospel on Good Friday, because that primacy helps to give the day and the liturgy its character. The tradition gave us Matthew's Passion on Palm Sunday. The current lectionary gives us Matthew, Mark and Luke in a three-year cycle. But for Good Friday we, like Egeria and her fellow pilgrims, are given John, different in mood and character. That does not only mean that we hear a slightly different version of the story, but that the whole celebration of the day has a different ethos. Essentially it is celebration ('celebration' is the right word) of the victory of Christ and the glory of the cross.

In John, the words of the dying Christ are 'It is finished.' The ordeal is over. He has gone through it all, save death itself, and that is now to take him over. He has walked the sorrowful way with passion and yet with dignity and it is over. 'It is finished.' And yet it is more than that. 'It is accomplished.' The Greek is almost 'It is consummated.' Something has been achieved, something immeasurable, something eternal, something that changes the whole relationship of the human race with its creator. The apostle Paul tells us that 'God was in Christ reconciling the world to himself' (2 Corinthians 5.19) and, though that process begins in the stable in Bethlehem, it reaches its climax on the hill outside Jerusalem. For John the cross is all accomplishment. It is not disaster, or failure or tragedy. It is the will of God and the means of the world's salvation. It is good news, gospel, for the human race. And so his account of the life and death of Jesus Christ is all about glory, but glory of a strange divine sort that the world fails to perceive. Jesus' path through human life is a triumphal procession revealing the glory of God, and the cross is the great climax, where the ultimate victory is won. 'I, lifted up from the earth, will draw everyone to myself' (John 12.32). As he hung upon the cross he had indeed drawn the whole world to himself.

This ancient liturgy, which was already acquiring its mood and shape in the fourth century, has John's perspective. For all the solemnity, for all the austerity, for all the deep emotions it can bring out, there is a quiet confidence and more than a hint of glory. We wait for Easter when the Risen Lord will be among his people, but we know that his victory does not delay till then. It is won high upon the cross, the world drawn to him, divine nature revealed, and humankind reconciled to God. The solemnity and the austerity have their place. The church is bare as it was at the end of Thursday evening, but the cross will be accompanied by lights when it is brought in. The ministers will not be in black, as if this were some kind of memorial service, but red, the colour not only of blood but of kingship. The music, though unaccompanied if possible, will not be funereal, but will 'sing the praise of him who died upon the cross'. That all reflects the Johannine perspective.

It is a liturgy that makes its impact through the proclamation of powerful scriptures and through two devotional actions. It is essentially a participative liturgy, for Good Friday does not, in the end, invite us to gaze on Christ, but to identify with him and share with him. It could not be more different from the three hours of sitting and listening passively.

Liturgy

The Liturgy of Good Friday in *Times and Seasons* has four main stages between the Gathering and the Dismissal. These are the Liturgy of the Word, the Proclamation of the Cross, the Prayers of Intercession and the Liturgy of the Sacrament. Depending on the musical resources and the number of participants it is a service that would naturally last between one and a quarter and one and a half hours if celebrated unhurriedly. Periods of silence are as important as any words or songs. *Times and Seasons* has this note.

> Silence is a significant part of the observance of Good Friday, and silence at the points indicated is integral to the service. It is appropriate for the organ to be used only to accompany singing. (p. 306)

The effectiveness of the liturgy depends in part on the simplicity of its music. Unaccompanied singing would be best of all.

The Gathering is simplicity itself. The ministers – essentially the president and a minister, ordained or lay, to be the deacon, though there could be other robed ministers – enter in silence and keep a time of silent prayer before the bare altar table. There is much to be said for everyone who is able, ministers and people, to kneel. The silent prayer leads into the Collect and then all sit for the Liturgy of the Word.

In a way the Liturgy of the Word does not differ from that on any Sunday. There are three readings provided, together with a psalm, the possibility of a hymn and the expectation of a sermon. But the scriptural texts today are more than usually crucial to the mood of the liturgy and require to be read with skill and sensitivity. The first reading is Isaiah 52.13 – 53.12, the 'suffering servant' passage that sets the scene for this liturgy in a telling way. There follows Psalm 22 (either the first 11 verses or the first 21), which begins with the cry 'My God, my God, why have you forsaken me?' and continues to resonate with the story of the passion. In places where singing would be difficult, the text needs to be read in whatever way will convey its pathos most clearly. The reading from Hebrews that follows is less crucial and, if one reading needs to be omitted, this is the one rather than the Isaiah passage. A time of silence should follow each reading.

The final reading is John's account of the Passion. The whole of chapters 18 and 19 are given and a shorter version loses something. Nevertheless 19.1–37 is the heart of the story. The different ways of proclaiming the Passion – sung or spoken, one voice, three voices or many voices, the congregation silent or speaking, standing or sitting – have all been discussed in Chapter 5 in relation to Palm Sunday and the same consider-ations apply here. Perhaps there is a case for a more austere and restrained rendering of it on Good Friday. Certainly there is case for using a different approach from that on Palm Sunday. The response to the Passion must be silence, even though a homily, however brief, ought to follow.

What follows now is the Proclamation of the Cross (though a note allows it to be later in the service after the Prayers of Intercession). Its origin lies in the devotional action described by Egeria, where the belief was that they were venerating a piece of the true cross, something we know is not available to us, though, as we saw, in Egeria's day it was a fairly informal business before the proper liturgy began. On Good Friday it is the most natural thing in the world to fix our eyes on the cross, to recognize it for the sign of victory that it is and to offer praise and thanksgiving for its meaning. What is needed is not a cross that is normally on the altar table or carried at the front of a procession, but a large impressive cross, perhaps heavy but not too much so, more likely rough-hewn than beautifully shaped and polished. Or it may be a crucifix with the figure of Christ upon it.

After the sermon the ministers go to the back, the liturgical west, of the church. If the church has acolytes' candles, they can be lit and carried high to accompany the cross as it is brought through the church. The president or the deacon carries the cross. It should be carried high as a sign of triumph, in line with the Johannine theology, not dragged along as if the min-ister carrying it were Jesus on the way to Golgotha. The cross is brought in slow procession through the church, stopping at three points. At each of these three points the congregation is encouraged to turn towards it. These words are sung or said:

The cross of Christ.
The cross on which the Saviour of the world was hung.

Or

This is the wood of the cross,
on which hung the Saviour of the world.
Come, let us worship.

The procession may be in silence, save for these words. But there is also the possibility of a hymn or song with the three 'stations' and the words that accompany them interspersed between the verses of the hymn. The traditional hymn is *Crux fidelis*, 'Faithful cross', the sixth-century hymn by Venantius Fortunatus, found in some hymn books as verses from the hymn 'Sing my tongue, the glorious battle'. There is a modern translation by Ralph Wright:

Sing in triumph of our Saviour,
raise your voices, sing with pride,
of the gentle one who loves us
and for us was crucified,
stretched upon the cross in torment,
healing hatred as he died.

Sing of gall, of nails, of spittle,
sing of sponge and spear and rod,
how the blows of soldiers opened
wounds within the heart of God,
and the world of pain found healing,
bathed within the Saviour's blood.

See the noble cross resplendent,
standing tall and without peer.
Where, O Tree, have you a rival
in the leaf or fruit you bear?

Sweet the burden, sweet the ransom,
that through iron your branches bear.

Bend your boughs, O tree, be gentle,
bring relief to God's own limbs,
bow in homage to bring comfort
to the gentle King of kings;
ease the throne where your creator
harshly treated, calmly reigns;

For of all the woods and forests
you were chosen out to hold
that fair prize that would win harbour
for a drifting, storm-tossed world;
you whose wood has now been purpled,
by the Lamb's own blood enfurled.

May our praises and our wonder
echo through the heart of light
to the Father who creates us
and the Son whose gentle might
in the Spirit won us freedom
from the grasp of endless night.
(*Hymns for Prayer and Praise 148*)

Where there is a choir, it might be sung with the verses alternating between the choir the and the whole community.

Verses from 'O sacred head' (*A&M* 181) are another possibility. But if musical resources are very limited it may be better not to sing during this procession with the cross lest people be more absorbed with words in a service book than looking at the cross.

When it has been brought in the cross needs to be placed prominently where it may dominate the remainder of the liturgy. If there have been lighted candles, they stand beside it. The cross needs a stand, so that it may be upright. In some settings it makes sense for it to be placed on the altar. It needs to be where people can draw near to it, where possible from all sides.

There follow two stages of response to the cross. The first is communal. There need to be texts and, if possible, songs, as the community turns towards the cross and gives thanks for the cross and for the Crucified One. *Times and Seasons* provides four texts (pp. 310–15), as well as mentioning the *Crux fidelis* text which can be used once the cross is in place if it has not been sung as it is brought through the church. The first provision is the 'Reproaches', given in two versions, though neither is the traditional form. Here is an area of sensitivity. A note throws light on why this is so.

> The Reproaches are not printed here in their traditional form. Where it is desired to use the traditional form, because (for example) the text is being sung to a well-known setting like that of Victoria or Sanders, it is important to remember that Jesus' words are to be understood as applying to the present Church, rather than to his own contemporaries. Here 'Israel' and 'my people' stand for the Church, and we are to hear the Reproaches as directed to our own hardness of heart and failure of discipleship. (p. 306)

The issue is the perceived anti-Semitism of the original text, which dates from the ninth century and which can be found in translation in the *New English Hymnal* (516). The two contemporary versions in *Times and Seasons* are very clearly addressed to the Church, rather than to the Jewish people, and thus avoid the charge of anti-Semitism. The other three 'anthems' are biblical texts with congregational responses, all briefer than the Reproaches, all equally appropriate as sung or spoken texts. If spoken, rather than sung, they might lead into a hymn.

But the second element of response to the cross can be more individual and personal. While hymns, anthems, songs or chants are sung quietly, people may be invited to come out of their seats, draw near to the cross and spend a moment in reflection, a moment of intimacy with the crucified Christ. The tradition that speaks most easily about the 'veneration' of the cross has at this point had people come to the cross and kiss the feet of the crucified figure on the cross or kiss the wood. But it does not have to be like that. People may simply come and kneel for a moment. Or stand in contemplation. Or touch the cross. Indeed not everybody has to do the same thing. People need to be comfortable with what they do, but it can be a profound moment for each person who draws near reflectively and prayerfully. It is another of those powerful experiences that can transform. It does not need to be neat and tidy and is better not so. It is not like queuing for Communion. That is why it is good if people can approach the cross from more than one direction. But it cannot be hurried. The ministers need to make this devotion first. It may be important to have a few others briefed to start the movement and to do different things, thus giving permission for others. When all who wish have done so, this part of the liturgy needs to conclude, perhaps with these words:

We adore you, O Christ, and we bless you,
because by your holy cross you have redeemed the world.

Or perhaps with a hymn. This could be the very best moment in the day for Isaac Watts' great hymn of the Passion, 'When I survey the wondrous cross' (*A&M* 157). But, however much singing and speaking is included in the Proclamation of the Cross, silence remains the key ingredient. This silence needs to be significant and to give character to this part of the service, not squeezed out by either words or music.

There follow now the Prayers of Intercession, the 'Solemn Prayers' as they are often called. In shape and to some extent in text they follow the deepest tradition of intercession, with a series of biddings, times of silence and collects. In subject matter they include, as usual, the needs of the Church and the world, of those who suffer and those who have died. But on this occasion they also focus on the relationship between Christians and Jews and on people of other faiths. The words in both these cases have been chosen with particular care and sensitivity. These prayers have a solemnity about them appropriate to the day. A temptation to substitute something lighter, briefer or more extempore is probably best resisted on this occasion. The traditional manner of praying these prayers is for a deacon to speak the biddings, the people to pray silently in response to the biddings and the president to say the collects. Where there is no deacon the biddings might be spoken by others in the community, but with the collects staying with the president. There is the sense of praying at the foot of the cross, so on this occasion it makes sense for the president (and the deacon if there is one) to be facing the cross. If there has been much kneeling during the Proclamation of the Cross there is an argument for these prayers to be said with everyone standing. But, as with much else in relation to posture, this is a matter for local decision.

Holy Communion

We come now to one of the key decisions in relation to Good Friday. Are people to be invited to receive Holy Communion as the final stage of this liturgy? If the answer is no, then, after the Solemn Prayers, the Lord's Prayer is said, perhaps a final hymn or song is sung, and after a single concluding prayer all depart in silence. But the case for Holy Communion is a strong one.

It is something of an accident that Holy Communion ceased to be part of Anglican experience on Good Friday. Communion on Good Friday from the 'reserved sacrament' (consecrated on Maundy Thursday) appears at Rome in the seventh and eighth centuries in 'both kinds' – consecrated bread and wine. From the ninth century only the consecrated host was reserved and not the consecrated wine, and there was a decline in the number of communicants in many places, though in some religious establishments general communion persisted. In the later Middle Ages the procession to and from the place of 'repose' became more and more elaborate, so that the Reformers, most of whom did not approve of the reserved sacrament in principle, decided that this was an aspect of liturgical tradition that had to go.

There remained the possibility of a full celebration of the Eucharist and indeed that is still permitted, though no special eucharistic texts are provided for Good Friday. Anglicans have not in general followed some Free Churches that have made a celebration of the Lord's Supper on Good Friday a feature of their worship. Indeed many Anglicans have come to describe the lack of Communion on Good Friday, not as a historically accidental omission, but as a principle. Sometimes they have seen it as a reflection of a sort to the words of Jesus that Luke gives at the Maundy Thursday supper:

> I have eagerly desired to eat this Passover with you before I suffer; for I tell you, I will not eat it until it is fulfilled in the kingdom of God. (Luke 22.15–16)

Somehow that becomes understood as a foregoing of Communion until Easter, when we are reunited with the Risen Christ. But that is not what Jesus said and by fulfilment in the kingdom of God he certainly did not mean the celebration of Easter. The key words to consider in relation to this subject are Paul's to the Corinthians:

> As often as you eat this bread and drink the cup, you proclaim the Lord's death until he comes. (1 Corinthians 11.26)

To share the bread and the cup is a powerful proclamation of the death of Christ. It also expresses our solidarity with him. If we are to look in the words of Jesus for a reference to eating and drinking with him, we are better going to his words to James and John:

'Are you able to drink the cup that I drink, or be baptized with the baptism that I am baptized with?' They replied, 'We are able.' Then Jesus said to them, 'The cup that I drink you will drink; and with the baptism with which I am baptized, you will be baptized.' (Mark 10.38f.)

Jesus is talking about Good Friday no more in this passage than he is doing so when he speaks of waiting for the kingdom of God. But his words about sharing his cup, the cup about which he has spoken in Gethsemane, have a particular poignancy and to share Communion on Good Friday is a natural expression of solidarity with him.

I confess that, having been brought up in a tradition of abstinence from Holy Communion on Good Friday, I took a long time to see its merits. For me that moment came when, as a parish priest, we welcomed to the parish as our Holy Week preacher a Franciscan friar who was passionate about the rightness of Holy Communion on Good Friday. Out of deference to him we decided to try it for one year. The moment of conversion – I put it as strongly as that – was when, as three o'clock, the hour of the death of Jesus, struck, those present had just come out of their seats and were kneeling on three sides of the sanctuary under the great wooden cross on the altar. It was for me as if everyone was saying, 'Lord, I identify with you, as far as I am able, I share your cup, I allow myself to be drawn into your passion.' Ever since then I have wanted Holy Communion on Good Friday and advocated it wherever I have been. In the few years that I have been in places where there was no Communion on Good Friday, I have yearned for it. For me it is, like the veneration of the cross, the embracing of Christ's way of living and dying, and thus a moment of transformation. I cannot advocate it too strongly.

Whereas in the Roman Catholic liturgy until 1955 it was only the priest who received Communion, contemporary practice is for all to receive, and obviously that would be the practice in an Anglican setting. In the Roman Catholic setting, it would usually be only the consecrated bread that was received, even by the priest. In the light of the discussion about 'the cup' above, it is clearly better for both consecrated bread and wine to be distributed.

To return to the order of service, if Holy Communion is to be received, after the Prayers of Intercession and perhaps during the singing of a hymn or song, a fair linen cloth is placed upon the altar table (in front of the cross if that has been placed there) and the consecrated elements brought reverently and placed upon it. The Lord's Prayer is said and the Invitation to Communion given. The Distribution follows. Although a rubric indicates that there may be hymns and anthems during the Distribution, there is also a case today for a silent Distribution, save for the ministers saying, 'The body of Christ, broken for you' and 'The blood of Christ, shed for you'.

After Communion any consecrated bread and wine that remains is consumed, a single prayer is said and, without Blessing or Dismissal, the ministers and the whole community depart in silence. The cross remains in place. If there are candles beside it, they remain alight.

When?

There has to be careful consideration of when to celebrate this principal liturgy on Good Friday. In places where people are unlikely to come in the middle of the day, there is the option of the morning (though it is odd to reach the moment of the death of Jesus at an early hour in the day) or the evening (if that is when people are available). In modern Roman practice, the liturgy begins at three o'clock, the hour of the death of Jesus. Anglicans more often work towards a liturgy that ends at or not long after that hour. This would suggest a two o'clock service or, if there is to be a lot of music and a large congregation participating in the veneration and in Communion, 1.30 pm.

There is also the possibility of absorbing the Liturgy into a variant on the traditional 'Three Hours' and this has become quite common. Beginning at 12 noon there is a series of readings, reflections, addresses, silences, songs and prayers until a longer time of silence before the Liturgy begins. There is a recognition that some people will arrive at 12, others over the next hour or so, with more arriving during the longer silence before the Liturgy, the time of which needs to be known. What is unhelpful is to advertise a Three Hours in which people will come, but also go, for this will mean that they may leave at the point when the reflection, essentially preparation, leads into the Liturgy, essentially the celebration. Best to arrive when they can, but then to stay till the end.

It has been outside the compass of this book to explore the place of children in the liturgy of Holy Week. There are many moments when they can be fully involved, as much caught up in the story and the liturgical actions as adults, and there are good resources to help their involvement. But Good Friday is a particular challenge, both because of the possible length of the Liturgy and also because of the long times of silence. Communities with the resources to do so have developed really worthwhile Good Friday projects that do indeed create activities for children through a whole three hours, exploring the whole Holy Week story with them and working also on art work that can be brought into the church for Easter. For all the benefits of all-age worship, this is one day when adults and children may have different needs to fulfil.

In terms of worship it remains only to look briefly, if the Liturgy has been completed by mid or late afternoon, at what other service there might be. One approach sees everything from the end of the Liturgy until Easter as a time of silent waiting, about which more in the following chapter, a kind of liturgical desert with no communal worship. Or there may be the saying of simple offices and *Common Worship, Daily Prayer* indicates a series of omissions that makes Morning and Evening Prayer more severe. But another possibility is to make

Evening Prayer on Good Friday a commemoration of the Burial of Christ. There is precedent for such an office and, as part of it, the 'burial' of the cross representing the body of Jesus. (In the Middle Ages there was also the 'burial' of the eucharistic host with much the same intention. This was unique to England and accounts for the 'Easter sepulchre' on the north side of the sanctuary of some medieval churches.) The austere form of Evening Prayer would include the account of the burial of Christ. The song 'Were you there when they crucified my Lord?' (A&M 184) might be sung unaccompanied, ending with the verse 'Were you there when they laid him in the tomb?' The cross would be taken down slowly from its place in the sanctuary and carried flat, like a coffin, by four people to the place that is to act as the tomb. I have known that to be a crypt chapel in one church, a normally unused north porch in another, a specially made 'tomb' in another. When the cross has been placed in the 'tomb', the minister closes the door or gate, capturing the moment of the burial of Jesus, and says a prayer usually associated with Night Prayer.

Lord Jesus Christ, Son of the living God,
who at this evening hour lay in the tomb
and so hallowed the grave to be a bed of hope
for all who trust in you:
give us such sorrow for our sins,
which were the cause of your passion,
that when our bodies lie in the dust,
our souls may live with you for ever.

It is a moment of finality that Easter will reveal to be a false ending, but for the moment it serves to help us into the place of desolation that those who buried Jesus felt, or into the place of hope and waiting that marks the Christian reflection on the words of the Creed: 'He descended into hell'.

So much for liturgical observance of Good Friday. But the instinct of witness outside the church building is a very good one and ought not to be lost in the recovery of better worship inside the church. It may be something as simple as the prominent display of a cross, perhaps decked with purple robe and crown of thorns, in the churchyard or another public place. But it could also be an outside Stations of the Cross, through the streets, or better still an imaginative representation of the Passion, telling the story to those who will not enter the church building. But it is participation in the liturgy that will best prepare people for such an effective act of witness. Worship and evangelism are both important responses to the cross.

8

Easter Eve

Character

Good Friday leads to Easter Eve, which is sometimes called 'Holy Saturday', but never 'Easter Saturday', for Easter has not yet begun. It is, like Good Friday, a day on which the Eucharist is not celebrated. Unlike Good Friday, it is also a day on which Holy Communion is never received. We will explore later the celebrating of the Easter Liturgy (with the Eucharist and the receiving of Communion) late on Saturday evening, but when that happens it arises from an understanding that with dusk on Saturday we have moved from Easter Eve to Easter Day.

One of the subtleties of Holy Week that we have been exploring is the way in which the liturgy each day has a twist at the end that moves our meditating, thinking and praying on to a new phase. On Palm Sunday we are not intended to go away still waving palms and singing hosannas. We read the Passion and move on so that the mood of Maundy Thursday and Good Friday is almost upon us. Then, on Maundy Thursday itself, we are not meant to slip home full of the warm glow of the fellowship in the upper room, but are confronted with the darkness and the night, the desolation and the betrayal.

What mood are we to take home on Good Friday? Of course we take home the cross, with its shame and glory, and all the deep emotions that we bring to the surface as we celebrate the passion. But, in a sense, what we also have to take is the space, the yawning gap, between that three o'clock on Friday afternoon and that event in the darkness of the night that links Saturday and Sunday, before dawn, when mysteriously, unwatched by human eyes, Jesus bursts the grave. That space, that yawning gap, has no liturgy. There is nothing, save the Church's daily prayer, stripped to its most austere, and Scripture, from the moment we celebrate the Lord's death until that moment when we celebrate the resurrection.

Scripture

It is worth pausing on the Scripture. First, there are the accounts of the burial of Jesus. All four tell essentially the same story, but with interesting details. The initiative for burying the body lies with Joseph of Arimathea. Matthew tells us that he was a disciple of Jesus, but John adds 'though a secret one for fear of the Jews'. Mark tells us that he was a respected member of the council, Luke that he was a good and righteous man, waiting for the kingdom of God. He goes to Pilate and requests the body. Mark notes that Pilate was surprised that Jesus was dead already. John records that Nicodemus, 'who had first come to Jesus by night', assisted with the anointing of the body and the burial. All four speak of the tomb, though only John tells us it was in a garden and Matthew alone tells us it was a tomb that Joseph had had made for his own burial. Matthew and Mark record the rolling into place of a great stone. All but John tell us about the women, who included Mary Magdalene and Mary the mother of Joses. They saw where Jesus was laid and the two Marys sat there for a while, as if still keeping the same vigil as they had kept at the foot of the cross. Matthew alone also goes on to tell how the priests went back to Pilate and requested soldiers to guard the tomb. Taking up their post, they sealed the stone (Matthew 27.57–66; Mark 15.42–47; Luke 23.50–56; John 19.38–42).

The lectionary allows for the reading of either Matthew's or John's version at the 'principal' service of Easter Eve, though John will almost certainly have been read on Good Friday afternoon or evening and, in a sense, Matthew's account is out of time, for it describes a Friday event, not a Saturday one. Saturday really is the day of the yawning gap. Some of the other scriptures help us reflect on the yawning gap.

The First Letter of Peter puzzles over the meaning of Jesus dead and buried, when it says:

> He was put to death in the flesh, but made alive in the spirit, in which also he went and made a proclamation to the spirits in prison. (1 Peter 3.18b–19)

The Apostles' Creed affirms something of the same truth, insisting, perhaps a little misleadingly, that 'he descended into hell'. Christian theology, at least in medieval times, developed that into a picture of Christ who 'harrows hell', who descends into hell and defeats the powers of evil; it is a favourite theme of art and drama in the Middle Ages. Here we are not only into a highly pictorial language, but into an area of theological speculation, unable to speak with precision about the nature of things the other side of death. But I suggest that some of the meaning of the space, the yawning gap, is not in a picture, but in the waiting.

Waiting

We have to enter imaginatively, if we can, into the mind of Christ, as we have done so many times in Holy Week. He has endured. He has accomplished. Death has done its worst and darkness has overwhelmed his soul. Does the desolation he has known in this life follow him to Hades? What is it like for Jesus in the place of the dead? We cannot know, at least not entirely. But we are not without clue. For in our human life we do experience moments of deep darkness that we believe are death-like. The end of a dream, the death of a loved one, a broken marriage or love affair, a painful ending to a friendship, a loss of freedom, even a loss of faith. All these are moments when life stands still, empty of meaning, robbed of all its familiarity and security. We are utterly exposed. This is the nearest most of us have ever come to an experience of death. And our exposure, our vulnerability and our numbness is a kind of nakedness akin to the nakedness of Christ as they took his bruised and broken body down from the cross. There is too a kind of nakedness of the soul.

In those experiences of darkness there is at first a sort of nothingness, an emptiness, a numbness. There is not even the desire to live again, to flourish again. There is no thought, to speak theologically, of resurrection. It is total darkness, not just over the land, but darkness in the soul. But there does come hope and salvation, sometimes long delayed, sometimes more speedily than we could have dreamed. Rarely is it instant. At first it is the smallest flickering light, the sense that we might come through; no more than that. But, often almost imperceptibly, something spells a glimmer of hope. A word from a friend, or even a stranger, a gesture of affection or compassion, a touch, a change of surroundings, a powerful remembering, a flood of tears. One of these, or something like it, introduces the possibility of new life, fresh beginning. The waiting has started. It is not that 'salvation' has arrived. It may be far away, and still long delayed. Or it may be three days away.

My theme has been that, when we look at Jesus and rehearse his story once again, we discover connections that make sense of our own story. As we reflect on the lifeless body of Jesus and the near silence of Scripture and the liturgy on the meaning of his being dead, we have to make connections. We ask what it was like for Jesus. In the experience of death, in the descending into hell, as the Creed puts it, was there for him the waiting and the yearning for the Father to act, the sense of light at the end of the tunnel, before ever the realization that the tunnel was but a tomb, and the love of the Father was stronger than death? Was it like this for Jesus as it was for Job in another of the readings for Easter Eve?

O that you would hide me in Sheol, that you would con-
ceal me until your wrath is past, that you would appoint
me a set time, and remember me! If mortals die, will they
live again? All the days of my service I would wait until my
release should come. (Job 14.13–14)

I do not know. But I suspect something like it if we are to make
sense of the space and the yawning gap. So we come back from
the experience of Jesus to ourselves and recognize how important it is that Easter Eve is not just a day off between Good
Friday and Easter Day, but is the day of waiting, as crucial as
the day of dying and the day of rising. The silence between the
shout of 'Crucify' and the Alleluia song is more than a void.
The silence is as significant as the song.

Liturgy?

Yet that is almost the hardest thing to communicate, for there
is, rightly, no great liturgy and the reality is that people are
not so much waiting as busying themselves in preparation for
Easter, not least in the church building itself, spring-cleaning
and flower arranging for the Easter festival. At least, for the
few who join in Morning and Evening Prayer, there is the possibility of that being conveyed by offices marked by silence and
the more than generous provision of readings for the day. (It is
difficult to know when the 'principal service' readings will be
used other than at Morning or Evening Prayer.) Perhaps, late in
the day, with the busyness over and the preparations done, the
community can gather to keep vigil, to discovering the meaning
in the waiting.

But here comes another issue. It is addressed mainly in the
following chapter. It is the issue of the Easter Liturgy. For the
Easter Liturgy is an event that begins in the Easter Eve experience of waiting and vigil, but ends in the Easter Day experience,
the waiting over, of being reunited with the Risen Lord. In the

next chapter we will explore the timing of the Easter Liturgy. May it be legitimately celebrated in its entirety after dark on the Saturday? My answer would be yes, but, if it is, by the time it finishes Easter has begun. Essentially it is not an Easter Eve service, but an Easter Day service brought back into the night.

There is a possibility of celebrating that liturgy in stages, keeping all that belongs properly to Easter till dawn or even mid-morning, but simply keeping a vigil of Scripture, silence, prayer and song on Saturday night, still within the mood of Easter Eve and an atmosphere of waiting. *Times and Seasons* provides 'The Vigil Readings, Psalms and Prayers' (pp. 375–97) and emphasizes the need for silence. Obviously there can also be hymns, songs and chants. The readings are not the same as provided for earlier in the day on Easter Eve. Those were concerned with Jesus dead and buried and waiting for the release of Easter. But the Vigil Readings explore the whole Bible story of redemption. Nevertheless, a well-paced Vigil in a darkened church captures helpfully the essential meaning of Easter Eve. However, once a paschal candle has been lit and an alleluia sung, Easter Eve has given way to Easter Day and that may not be what we want on the day of waiting. It may be better to return home still in the darkness, but now, having heard the stories of God's saving acts in history, a darkness filled with hope and expectancy for tomorrow, the day of resurrection.

9

Easter Liturgy

Origins

It is an extraordinary and deeply disappointing thing that the liturgy that scholars regard as the celebration that captures the meaning of the death and resurrection of Jesus more than any other, and that has swept off their feet many who have participated in it in all its richness, is unknown to the majority of English churchgoers. As was described at the beginning of this book, in most places it has simply not been celebrated or it has been something for a pious minority either on Saturday evening or at dawn on Sunday, while most churchgoers have waited for mid-morning and for something not unlike what they do from week to week.

As we have seen, before ever there was a Holy Week, a Palm Sunday or a Good Friday, there was Easter and a single unitive service that told the story of God's saving activity in history culminating in the story of the passion and the resurrection of Christ. It began after dusk, it continued through the night, it reached the Easter story of Jesus coming forth from the tomb at sunrise. It was the principal, though not the only, occasion in the year for the baptism of new Christians and it concluded with the Eucharist in which the newly baptized participated and in which everyone present was reunited with their Lord who had gone through death and emerged victorious. There are communities where such a liturgy, beginning in the evening darkness and ending in the morning light, is possible, but not many. For most there has to be some compromise, some making of choices, that can make the liturgy manageable for contemporary Christians and enable it to be the Easter celebration *par excellence* in every community, but only, of course, if it is worth it.

It is worth it. It is worth struggling with all the issues that get in the way of its effective celebration. There are enough people who will give their witness to the life-transforming experience of this liturgy of fire, light, water, bread and wine, of musical instruments and bells, of long silences and cascades of alleluias. It needs to be experienced by all the others who hardly know of its existence.

Times and Seasons, which in relation to the rest of Holy Week has done little more than update the liturgies that were first published in *Lent, Holy Week, Easter*, has treated the Easter Liturgy very differently. It has unpacked the provision, provided detail, explored a variety of approaches, all in the interest of showing how this liturgy can enrich the worship of every church, not only parishes with rich resources and a catholic tradition. If anyone is still reluctant, let them cast aside their reluctance and explore something that might change the community and its worship, not just for a day, but for years to come.

When?

The Easter Liturgy has four elements. One is a Service of Light, at the heart of which is the lighting of a great candle that will symbolize throughout Eastertide the presence of the Risen Lord. A second is a Liturgy of the Word which, unless it is reduced to a minimum, includes a number of readings from the Old Testament, together with songs, silences and prayers, and is called a Vigil. In some communities the whole service is called 'The Easter Vigil', but that name is better reserved for this particular part of the service. The order of the first two – Service of Light and Vigil – can be reversed. A third element is a Liturgy of Baptism or, if there are no baptismal candidates, at least a remembrance of Baptism at the font. A fourth is the Eucharist from the Peace to the Dismissal.

There are a number of principles to bear in mind in relation to the Easter Liturgy. By far the most important is that it should be celebrated at an hour when the community can and will come together in good numbers.

There are places where many people are ready to rise with the dawn or a little before the dawn. If so, that is a very good time for the Easter Liturgy, but if only a handful of people will come and most will wait for a later celebration, it is not a good time. There are places where people will come at midnight, as they do at Christmas, in which case that can be a good time, though such a service loses the element of ending in the morning light of Easter Day.

There are probably rather more places where, if the service is marketed well, people are willing to come in good numbers on Saturday evening after dusk. Not everybody is happy in principle with this as it means proclaiming the resurrection and possibly receiving Easter Communion before midnight. However, as was mentioned in the previous chapter, such a practice makes good sense if one recognizes that, for the Jewish people and for the Gospel writers, 'the third day' began with dusk on Saturday. There is nothing magic about midnight. We do not know at what hour Jesus came out of the tomb. We do know it was before the women came very early in the morning while it was still dark. So a Saturday night celebration can be a genuine and legitimate Easter celebration. It does have the advantage also over the dawn alternative that people are much more likely to return for a mid-morning service on Sunday to welcome others who have not shared in the earlier Liturgy.

There will be other places where a realistic assessment will recognize that Saturday evening, midnight and Sunday daybreak will all attract only a small number of the regular congregation, let alone those who come only for great festivals. In those circumstances it may be right to celebrate as much of the Easter Liturgy as possible in the usual Sunday mid-morning service. (In some rural benefices, of course, some churches may have to wait till Sunday afternoon or evening, but the same applies – use the Liturgy at whatever hour makes sense.)

The key decision is a pastoral one. What is the hour when the whole church community can gather in order to experience something breath-taking and transforming? That is much more important than any liturgical purity about whether one time is more authentic than another. Something of the same pastoral instinct has to come also into whether the liturgy is celebrated in one unitive service or whether different parts need to happen at different times from one another. It is a principle that the four parts belong together and ought to remain so whenever possible. But the primary pastoral principle may sometimes mean that they have to be divided.

It is possible to detach the Vigil of Readings and to have a reflective service of waiting on the evening of Easter Eve without too great a loss, as discussed in the previous chapter. The difficulty comes when this is combined with the Service of Light, for that part of the Liturgy explicitly proclaims the resurrection. The Easter acclamation is used, the Gloria is sung, bells are rung, the organ sounds forth. Easter has begun and, if it has begun, it is strange and rather unsatisfactory not to press on to the climax which is the encounter with the Risen Christ in the breaking of bread. So, in some ways, it is a particularly unsatisfactory division that celebrates the whole Liturgy except the Eucharist on Saturday night, keeping only the Eucharist for Sunday morning, though *Times and Seasons* permits it. On the other hand, the Service of Light clearly loses something, though not everything, if it happens mid-morning rather than at night.

Patterns

Once decisions have been made about when to celebrate the Easter Liturgy, a second choice has to be made. *Times and Seasons* sets out very clearly the two different patterns that can be adopted when using the full rite, Pattern A in which the Service of Light comes first, Pattern B in which the Vigil precedes the Service of Light. Both are very ancient patterns and both can make sense in a contemporary setting. In planning the service it is important to be clear from the start which is to be followed.

The more familiar to most who know the Easter Liturgy is Pattern A. It is the order in the Roman Missal. Here the service begins dramatically with the Service of Light, with fire and candle, and then settles down to the Vigil of Old Testament material, read by the light of the Easter Candle, giving way after the Easter acclamation and the Gloria to the New Testament reading and the Gospel before moving to the Liturgy of Baptism and thence on to familiar ground from the Peace. *Times and Seasons* explains this pattern in these terms:

> Here, the resurrection is proclaimed from the outset in the Service of Light. The Easter Candle, together with the candles held by the individual worshippers, should, if possible, illuminate the church. This illustrates the way that Christians understand the Old Testament and interpret life itself in the light of the resurrection of Jesus. The history of our salvation in the Scriptures is heard in the light of the Easter mystery. The Service of Light reaches its climax with the Easter Proclamation. (p. 324)

The Old Testament readings from the Vigil then follow. We hear the story of our salvation and are invited to reflect on our own personal journey in the light of the Easter revelation.

Pattern B begins without fire and Paschal Candle, though there will have to be a light for reading in what will otherwise be a Vigil in the dark, possibly ending with a Passion reading. Only when it has traced the story of redemption to that point does it begin the Easter celebrations with the Liturgy of Light, into which is inserted the initial part of the Liturgy of Baptism, before moving speedily on via the Easter Acclamation to the Gloria. This has historical precedent, indeed it is probably the earlier of the two patterns, but requires some rethinking by those used to the more familiar Pattern A. *Times and Seasons* says this about Pattern B:

> In the earliest forms of Easter Vigil the Old Testament Scriptures were read and reflected upon, until the resurrection was proclaimed in the Eucharist at cockcrow. This tradition forms the basis of Pattern B, which follows a storytelling approach.
>
> Pattern B begins with the lighting of a small fire or light by which the story of salvation is read. However, this light is *not* the Easter light and all effort should be made to avoid any confusion with it.
>
> The story of salvation is told through Old Testament readings selected from the vigil readings. Each reading adds to the story and a sense of expectation gradually increases until the service reaches its climax in the revelation of the resurrection. (p. 324)

Preparation

Whichever pattern is adopted, there is much preparation to be done before the liturgy can begin. *Times and Seasons* engages with the detail of the planning much more in relation to Easter than to the other liturgies of this week and so there is less need for detail in this book. Preparation will include the provision of fire, candles, tapers, a book of readings that can be read in a darkened building, the best white or gold vestments, water in and for the font, a branch of rosemary to sprinkle the people, the holy oils if there is to be Baptism or Confirmation, as well as appropriate music for every stage of the rite. There may also have been an invitation to those who will be present to bring hand bells and musical instruments. This will all be in addition to the preparation of the building for the Easter season, with a desire to make a contrast with the austerity of Lent and Good Friday by filling the church with flowers, banners, candles and signs of resurrection, which may include an Easter Garden.

Crucial to the preparation is careful thought about light and darkness. It is undesirable for people to arrive for the Liturgy and, because the preparations are still going on, to find the church flooded in light and full of Easter glory. The building needs to be in near darkness by the time the first worshippers are likely to arrive. There is the need also to ensure that, when words are to be spoken or sung by ministers and readers while the church is lit only by candlelight, there will be sufficient light to allow them to speak or sing their words confidently without stumbling. At the point before the Gloria when the church is to be flooded in light, work needs to have been done to ensure that it is as dramatic as possible, clearly easier in churches with dimmer switches, but important everywhere. One person responsible for 24 light switches in four different places in the church will not be able to do this well! As for the new fire, whether a small fire in a brazier or something more substantial, that needs to be delegated to someone with skill as much as enthusiasm if its lighting and that of the Easter Candle is not to degenerate into farce.

The most important light is, of course, the Easter or Paschal Candle. It is the primary symbol of the Risen Christ and serves as such through the 50 days till Pentecost. It is therefore important that it is not minimalist. It should dominate the celebration. It needs to stand taller than the other candles in the church. It needs its own space. Its candle-stand should be dignified and perhaps decorated with flowers. For the Easter Liturgy the Easter Candle should be positioned so that the *Exsultet* and the readings (following Pattern A) are read below its light, symbolically at least read by its light. For this reason it may be best placed by the pulpit and the *Exsultet* and the readings proclaimed from there. For the rest of Eastertide it may stand in any space where it is highly visible during worship. *Times and Seasons* provides guidance on marking it and inserting nails or studs representing the five wounds of Christ (pp. 408f.).

There is a particularly important issue if several churches come together for the Easter Liturgy in the evening or at dawn. If the Candle is the symbol of the Risen Christ, there must only be one. A collection of Easter candles (probably of different lengths) would be a nonsense. A note indicates that 'if it is desired to take Easter Candles back to other churches, they may be lit from the first candle at the end of the service and carried in procession out of the building' (p. 331), but even that introduces the confusion of more than one Risen Christ. Better that light should be taken from the Easter Candle and transported within a lamp by members of the congregation to the other churches where their Easter Candles can be lit.

Crucial to the preparation will also be decisions about personnel. Traditionally the Easter Liturgy has, in addition to a priest who presides, a deacon, who carries the Easter Candle and proclaims the resurrection in the *Exsultet* song. A second minister is certainly an advantage in this service. If it can be someone who is a deacon, all the better. If it can be someone who can sing, all the better. Such a person is desirable, but not essential. What is essential is a series of able well-rehearsed readers to bring to life the passages of Scripture, as well as people ready to shepherd and guide the congregation, who will be moving hither and thither as the liturgy proceeds, and to ensure their candles are lit at the right moments.

It is time to explore in a little more detail the four stages of the Easter Liturgy. For this purpose I am assuming Pattern A and a full celebration that includes all the elements, including the Eucharist. But clearly adjustments can be made where there are departures from this norm.

Service of Light

Essential to the Service of Light is the lighting of the Easter Candle, the symbol of the Risen Christ, the spreading of light through the congregation from that one source and the proclamation of the resurrection in the ancient song, *Exsultet*.

Ideally everyone gathers outside, each with a service order and a candle. If that is impractical, the ministers may be just outside the building or in the church porch while the congregation is gathered inside and turns to face the door. The president introduces the service on 'this most holy night when our Lord Jesus Christ passed from death to life'. The fire is kindled and a prayer of blessing said. The Easter Candle is marked, the 'nails' inserted and the Candle lit, with words provided for every stage. The Easter Candle, once alight, carried by the deacon, heads a procession into the church. Everyone follows and the light from the Candle is shared. Three times, as the procession moves through the church the deacon says or sings 'The light of Christ' and three times everyone replies 'Thanks be to God.' Especially if the congregation has been outside, but in any case because of the lighting of the candles, progress is very slow, but that is appropriate, for the truth that the light is overcoming the darkness and life overcoming the shadow of death takes time to make its impact.

There follows the *Exsultet*, so named for its first word in Latin, 'Rejoice', which is repeated at the beginning of the second and third stanzas. This 'Easter Song of Praise' or 'Paschal Proclamation' goes back to the seventh or eighth century, though there have been textual variants over the centuries. In its purest form it is a song sung simply by the deacon to a chant unique to the *Exsultet* and the role of the congregation is to listen, in wonder and joy, speaking only to respond to the familiar invitations to 'Lift up your hearts' and to 'give thanks to the Lord our God', clutching their candles as the deacon proclaims that 'this is the night', indeed 'most blessed of all nights', in which Christ rose from the dead. It is also a blessing of the Candle. The deacon sings:

Therefore, heavenly Father, in this our Easter joy
accept our sacrifice of praise,
your Church's solemn offering.
Grant that this Easter Candle may make our darkness light.
(p. 359)

Through the voice of an accomplished singer this long chant is a moment of great beauty. But in some places it will be too long as a monologue and in some places there will not be a singer of sufficient competence. There are a number of ways to make it more accessible. The first is a metrical version of the opening three stanzas – 'Sing, choirs of heaven! Let saints and angels sing!' (p. 358) – which can be sung to tunes of 10.10.10.10 metre, of which 'Woodlands' is the most obvious. The second is to use a metrical version for congregational singing of the whole *Exsultet,* and one is provided (p. 414). The third is to add a congregational response, 'Glory to you for ever', sung or spoken at the end of every paragraph. The fourth is to use a shorter and more contemporary text, and two are provided (pp. 413 and 416f.). Something is lost if the role of the deacon is entirely lost, but in many places something is gained if the stanzas alternate between the deacon and the congregation. Those with an eye to tradition will also be pleased to find a version that restores the reference to the bees that modern versions have generally suppressed.

> As we gaze upon the splendour of this flame
> fed by melting wax conceived by mother bee,
> grant that this Easter Candle may make our darkness light.
> (p. 412)

It should be noted that, using Pattern B, this entire section comes after the 'Vigil' and also that the Decision by Baptism candidates, the Renewal of Baptismal Vows by the congregation and the Signing with Cross on the foreheads of the candidates happens gathered around the 'new fire' after the Candle has been blessed but before it is brought through the church.

Vigil

We turn now to the Vigil. In Pattern A the church is lit by candlelight and each person is holding their lighted candle. The president introduces the Vigil and all sit and settle for the readings. Twenty-two readings are provided from which a selection will be made. At minimum there should be three, one of which ought to be the account of creation, and another of which must be the exodus crossing of the Red Sea. The third might be Noah and the flood, the valley of dry bones, the three young men in the burning fiery furnace or Jonah and the fish. It is a pity to have to choose. Each needs to be read by someone of real ability and each needs to be followed by a significant silence. Portions of psalmody are provided, but many places will want to vary the musical response to each reading. Depending on the musical resources, there may be a psalm after one, a chant after another, an anthem after another, a hymn after another, but preferably without instrumental accompaniment, which waits until later. The Vigil needs to end with a longer silence, out of which will come the Easter Acclamation. In my view the Taizé chant,

Bless the Lord, my soul, and bless God's holy name.
Bless the Lord, my soul, who leads me into life. (*A&M* 600)

leads effectively into that silence.

Now comes the last of the great turning points. The *Exsultet* has quite gently given us the good news that Christ is risen, but in such a restrained way that we have not yet 'let rip', so to speak. We have not responded with unadulterated Easter joy. But now comes the moment to do so. Out of the silence comes the first use of the Easter Acclamation.

Alleluia. Christ is risen.
He is risen indeed. Alleluia.

A note (p. 332) suggests that it might be used three times, first in a whisper, then louder and finally in a great shout. It is the moment when Easter has really arrived. A rubric (p. 338) adds that 'a joyful fanfare may be played, bells rung, cymbals clashed, noise made', though people are holding candles, so some things are difficult. This is the moment when the church is flooded in light and, if there is an organ, especially one that has been silent since Maundy Thursday, it thunders. Hand bells in the congregation are shaken and bells in the belfry ring out. There is a wonderful cacophony that gradually gives way to the introduction to the Gloria. The rubric (p. 338) suggests that this is the moment to extinguish the handheld candles, but it may be better to wait until after the Gloria and the Collect. A church that usually says, rather than sings, the Gloria needs to find a metrical version tonight. Speaking, rather than singing, will not catch the mood. The Collect follows.

This is the moment when people will probably extinguish their candles and sit. Paul's words to the Romans relating baptism to the death and resurrection of Christ are read (Romans 6.3–11), after which there may be Psalm 114, with an alleluia response, though more likely a hymn with alleluias, and the Gospel reading follows. There is an alleluia text more complex than usual to precede the Gospel. The alleluias here, as at the Easter Acclamation, need to be said or sung with particular joy as they return after their absence through Lent and Passiontide. The Gospel stays with the preferred Gospel for each year – Matthew 28.1–10 in Year A, Mark 16.1–8 in Year B and Luke 24.1–12 in Year C. The Fourth Gospel account is kept for another celebration. There is then provision for a sermon. If this is happening late in the evening or at dawn, it is probably not going to be a long one.

Initiation

The liturgy then moves on to the Liturgy of Initiation. At its least this will involve blessing water at the font and renewing the Profession of Faith. In its fullest form it will include not only Baptism, but also Confirmation, if there is a bishop to preside. If possible the whole community moves to the font. At

very least the ministers and candidates move there and the congregation turns towards the font. The Easter Candle, carried by
the deacon, leads this procession. It would be possible to relight
everyone's candles at this point, but it is not necessary. If the
procession to the font involves more than a few steps, there
needs to be a suitable hymn, chant or song, or litany. *Times
and Seasons* provides the 'Thanksgiving for the Resurrection'
(pp. 421–3).

If there are candidates for Baptism, they are presented at
this point. They may give their testimony. The whole community is asked whether it will uphold them. The candidates are
then asked the questions of the Decision, which also forms
the Renewal of Baptismal Vows by the remainder of the congregation. Candidates and congregation may speak together,
but it is also possible to have the congregation speak after the
candidates in relation to each question, in a kind of echo, so
that, for instance in relation to the first question, it proceeds
like this.

Do you reject the devil and all rebellion against God?
Candidates   I reject them.
All   **I reject them.**

If there are candidates they are signed with the cross. Water
is poured into the font with panache and the president prays
the Prayer over the Water, during which there is an optional
congregational acclamation sung or said. The community then
completes its Renewal of Baptismal Vows and any candidates
make their Profession of Faith in the words of the Apostles'
Creed. Baptism follows. Whether there have been candidates
or not, the president now sprinkles the whole community
with water from the font. The president might say repeatedly
'Remember your baptism into Christ Jesus.' If numbers allow,
an alternative is for each member of the congregation to go to
the font and make the sign of the cross on their forehead with
the water. The president adds a prayer.

If the bishop is presiding and there are candidates for Confirmation, the bishop confirms them now at the font. If there have been candidates for either Baptism or Confirmation a Commission may follow and, if candidates have been baptized, there is a Welcome to them. The Peace, which follows with an Easter text and alleluias, is formally part of the next part of the service, the Liturgy of the Eucharist, but it naturally happens around the font before people return and the focus moves to the altar table.

Eucharist

With the Liturgy of the Eucharist we are back on more familiar ground. If space allows it would be good if the community could now gather around the table, rather than return to the places they occupied earlier, but that will depend on local circumstances. We are not very adventurous in gathering communities like a crowd, whether around a font or an altar, and too many of our churches have too many immovable furnishings in the way to make this possible. But where it can be done, the occupying of a new space signifies a new stage in the Liturgy and the final stage of the journey that began on Ash Wednesday and ends now in being reunited with the Risen Lord in the breaking of bread.

The Eucharist follows its usual shape and most of the texts are familiar. The extended preface speaks of 'this night of our redemption'. There is a special text for the Breaking of the Bread. The Easter invitation to Communion, with its alleluias, is used for the first time. Surprisingly, the words recommended at the Distribution are the same as on Good Friday. In celebrating the resurrection, 'The body/blood of Christ keep you in eternal life' would seem a better option. After Communion there is a single prayer, the Easter Acclamation once again, a solemn Trinitarian blessing, the Giving of a Lighted Candle to anyone newly baptized and the Easter Dismissal with its double alleluias. No doubt somewhere there will also have been another Easter hymn with cascades of alleluias.

The ministers and people disperse, the Easter Candle remains in its place still burning. People may be encouraged to relight their own candles and take the paschal light home. As mentioned before, where the Easter Liturgy has been shared by more than one church, at this point the light needs to be taken back to the other churches. Appropriate now would be the ringing of the church bells, if it is dark possibly fireworks, almost certainly sparkling drinks.

Although *Times and Seasons* states that 'the Easter Eucharist may follow immediately on the Vigil, or be deferred until Easter Day' (p. 323), it also asserts that 'the celebration of the Eucharist is the proper climax to the Easter Liturgy when we are sacramentally reunited with our risen Lord' (p. 327). It is my strong conviction that this is so and that there is something profoundly unsatisfactory about proclaiming that Christ is risen, renewing vows at the font, joining in the Easter Acclamation, but then stopping the momentum of the liturgy in its tracks and going home without sharing in the breaking of bread. On the few occasions that I have had to do that, I have gone home somewhat at a loss.

During the day

Let us now imagine what might happen if there is no Saturday night service and no dawn service on Easter Day and that the decision has been taken to celebrate as much as possible of the Easter Liturgy mid-morning on Easter Day. How much of the Easter Liturgy can transfer to that later time? That will depend partly on how long or short the service needs to be, which will itself depend on the likely number of communicants. *Times and Seasons* gives some guidance, though there is more that can be said.

Much of the Service of Light can be used as it stands. References to 'this night' need to become 'this day' or 'this feast'. The president's introduction needs to be replaced by a less formal welcome. The fire can still be lit. More importantly, the Easter Candle can still be marked, blessed, lit and processed through the church. Everyone can have lighted candles. The *Exsultet* might need a little editing, but not a great deal.

The Vigil does not really transfer to mid-morning, more because of the time factor than any other reason. But it would be possible and desirable to use the Exodus reading (14.10–end) as the First Reading at the Eucharist and the Romans (6.5–11) as the Second. The Easter Acclamation, the Gloria and the Collect would follow straight after the *Exsultet*. The Liturgy of Initiation can be used unchanged and certainly the Renewal of Baptismal Vows should be included. The Liturgy of the Eucharist needs no change except the reference to 'night' in the Preface. If at all possible, a community that has had no service before the mid-morning of Easter Day should settle for little less than this.

Of course there will be communities that have celebrated the Liturgy in the night or in the very early morning but still want to repeat some of the Liturgy in a later service. The following chapter will address that and other possibilities for Easter Day.

10

Easter Day

Scripture

Because in following the lectionary we read the Scriptures in bite-sized portions we can miss the sense of pace and development of Easter Day. The Gospel accounts, for all that they have key truths in common, are distinctive. Mark might be said to short-change us, leaving us puzzled. Matthew tells us more about the guards than the disciples. But both Luke and John take us stage by stage through an overwhelming day of revelation.

John has Mary Magdalene alone going to the tomb early in the morning while it is still dark. She finds the stone rolled away and goes to tell Peter and 'the other disciple, the one whom Jesus loved', who race to the tomb. Peter is outrun by his companion, but goes into the tomb first and sees the linen cloths, but Jesus gone, though it is the other disciple who believes first. Then, rather surprisingly, the two return 'to their homes'. But Mary stands outside the tomb, weeping, and there follows that most beautiful of all Easter stories where she meets the Risen Lord, at first mistaking him for the gardener, but then recognizing him as her teacher. He sends her to tell the brothers that he is ascending 'to my Father and your Father, to my God and your God'. Mary does this, tells them she has seen the Lord. The scene moves to evening, but it is still Easter Day. The disciples are meeting behind locked doors (for fear of the Jews) when Jesus appears to them, shows them his hands and his side, greets them with his familiar 'Peace be with you' and breathes the Holy Spirit on them. All that on Easter Day, disciples coming and going and telling, Jesus appearing, reassuring, sending, breathing (John 20.1–23).

Luke has even more. It is a larger company of women (including Mary Magdalene, Joanna and Mary the mother of James) who go the tomb 'at early dawn'. They too find the stone rolled away, but meet two men in dazzling clothes who tell them Jesus has risen. They go to tell the disciples, who dismiss their report as an idle tale. But Peter believes sufficiently to go to the tomb to find out for himself. He sees the linen cloths, but, consistently with John's account, he goes home. The scene moves to the road from Jerusalem to Emmaus. Two disciples find a stranger joining them on the road and soon explaining the Scriptures to them. Reaching their village they invite him into their home for a meal and, as he takes the bread, blesses and breaks, suddenly they recognize him – 'It is the Lord!' But he has disappeared. Back to Jerusalem they go, bursting with their good news, only to discover that the disciples have already heard that Peter had met with Jesus. They are still talking about it, when Jesus himself appears to them all, with his 'Peace be with you'. He eats with them, explains the Scriptures to them, instructs them to wait in the city until they 'have been clothed with power from on high'. All this on Easter Day (Luke 24.1–49).

Of course Matthew tells us less, though in his account two Marys actually see the stone rolled away by an angel. Guards 'shook and became like dead men' at the sight, before going to the priests where a story is concocted that the disciples have stolen the body (Matthew 28.1–15). Mark tells us least of all, only that a 'young man, dressed in a white robe' told the women that Jesus was risen, but that they repeated the news to no one, for terror and amazement had seized them and they were afraid (Mark 16.1–8).

It is too easy on Easter Day to fix on just two pictures, an empty tomb and an appearance to Mary Magdalene, and to allow the other stories to wait until later in Eastertide. Indeed part of the function of Eastertide is to allow time to reflect on these over a period of time. But it is also helpful to capture this sense of a mystery that unfolds – a day of angels, encounters, messages, journeys, appearances and meal – and so to be swept off one's feet by it all. That is what the liturgy has to do on Easter Day – to sweep us off our feet, thrilled by the paschal mystery and wanting, like Mary Magdalene, Peter and the other disciples, to be reunited with the Risen Lord. Overwhelming wonder, joy and festivity are the marks of the day.

Liturgy

As has been said in the previous chapter, the church building will be vibrant with the golds and whites of a festival, with flowers, banners, candles and signs of resurrection. There are three particular artefacts that enhance the celebration – the Easter Candle, the font and the Easter Garden. More will be said about these in the following chapter, for they should continue to provide foci right through the Easter season. But today they are key – the Candle at the head of any procession and put in a place where it may dominate the liturgy, the font as the focus of the renewal of baptismal vows with generous sprinkling or splashing of water, the Garden with a potential to be a visual image of the story of Easter Day.

Times and Seasons makes generous provision for Easter Day. And it does, like all Anglican provision, speak consistently of 'Easter Day', not of 'Easter Sunday'. It provides an outline for a fairly informal open air Dawn Service, incorporating some elements of the Easter Liturgy following Pattern B. However, if this is a service attended by a smaller number than the mid-morning service, and especially if it is not (as seems likely) a celebration of the Eucharist, it may be better to adopt a different model and order and save the elements of the Easter Liturgy for incorporation in the mid-morning celebration.

If we move to mid-morning, there is the possibility of making this the moment when the Easter Liturgy is celebrated as fully as makes sense in daylight and with time constraints. *Times and Seasons* provides for this and it has been fully explored in Chapter 9. But what of communities that *have* celebrated the Easter Liturgy in the evening or at midnight or at dawn? What can they do to enhance a later mid-morning celebration, probably with a larger and mainly different congregation? *Times and Seasons* describes 'An Outline Service of the Word for Easter Day' (p. 404), but it also notes the canonical requirement to celebrate Holy Communion on Easter Day in every church (p. 327). We should do nothing to discourage people from coming to Holy Communion on this festival. Indeed it is the one day of the year that the Book of Common Prayer places them under an obligation to do so.

Much more likely is another Eucharist, with something of a different flavour than that in the Easter Liturgy. The use of the John Gospel in its longer form (John 20.1–18) with the meeting with Mary Magdalene contributes to that change. Especially with the Gospels of Matthew and Mark, the Liturgy at night has the mood of a cosmic earth-shattering event, whereas the morning Eucharist with John strikes more of a note of personal encounter with the Risen Christ. The Acts reading is one of the few that does not vary from year to year. It is part of the story of Peter and Cornelius that itself witnesses tellingly to the resurrection faith.

It would be wrong at such a service to repeat the lighting of the Easter Candle. But the service could well begin with the Easter Acclamation three times (getting louder each time) and a procession with the Candle brought through the congregation during the singing of 'Jesus Christ is risen today' or another alleluia hymn. Today of all days the Gospel reading needs cascades of alleluias sung to herald its reading. After the sermon there could be a movement to the font for the Renewal of Baptismal Vows and the sprinkling of the congregation. (If that takes place, the prayers of penitence may be omitted as well as the Nicene Creed.) The Easter form of the Peace and the Invitation to Communion are obviously suitable. Two things may be said about the beautiful Extended Preface. First, on Easter Day itself the fourth line should be changed from 'and in these days of Easter' to 'and on this feast of our redemption'. Second, throughout the season the line 'restored in men and women the image of your glory' should be amended to 'restored in men and women and children the image of your glory'. The omission of children has often been noted by children. Children might also gather with the ministers at the Easter Garden for the final prayers, the Solemn Blessing and the Easter Dismissal.

Resurrection

The underlying theme of this book has been that individuals and communities can be changed and transformed by walking with Jesus Christ through the events of Holy Week. That change and transformation may come dramatically at one of the profound moments in the week and in the story. More likely it will be happening gradually. Indeed it may be happening over years, as the individual or the community learns to go a little deeper each time the annual celebration of Holy Week comes round. But it may not happen until the week has reached its climax, which is not, in the end, at a hilltop crucifixion scene and not even in a garden staring into an empty tomb, but in an encounter with the Risen Jesus, which turns out to be a moment of resurrection as much for them as for Jesus. Sometimes the word 'transformation' gives way to 'resurrection'.

The resurrection of Jesus was unique, the divine reversal of the death on the cross, though, as we have seen, John in the Fourth Gospel can see the seeds of glory and triumph even on the cross.

Unless a grain of wheat falls into the earth and dies, it remains a single grain; but if it dies, it bears much fruit. (John 12.24)

Now, on Easter Day, we can picture Peter and the other disciple coming to the tomb, running towards the evidence of that triumph. For the grave is empty and they will find the Lord elsewhere, very much alive, breathing into them his Spirit. Though the resurrection of Jesus was unique, it shows a pattern. It reveals the way God works. Resurrection is what God does. The readings of Easter Day speak of Peter. Peter who, with his friends, had run away in the garden, had three times denied his Lord in the high priest's house, who, when the Beloved Disciple and the women stood at the foot of the cross, was nowhere to be seen. The events of that night and that day were for Peter a kind of death. But Peter, this broken man, is one of the first to find the tomb empty, and is the first to risk going into it; and maybe in that moment, with all its puzzlement (for John tells us that they did not understand the Scripture), were the seeds of new life for him. A little later Jesus will build on that and draw out of Peter affirmations of love that will wipe away three denials. Peter, who had descended into a hell of his own making, is drawn out of it by the Risen Lord. It is the resurrection of Peter. The resurrecting God is at work again, for this is the way God is. But Peter had to experience all the negativity, the knowledge that he had failed, in order to embrace a new life beyond anything he could have envisaged. The Christian who goes with Christ into the darkest places of Holy Week can also embrace a new life beyond imagining.

The Easter Day story moves from Peter to Mary Magdalene. Here is the woman whose life had gone wrong, whom Jesus had raised up, bringing her to life and accepting her love. But then that coming alive had gone wrong. He had been put to death and she had witnessed it. Now she goes to anoint his dead body. Life and love have fled. No wonder she weeps. But then, wonderfully, she meets the Risen Lord. She hears her name and in that moment the resurrecting God is at work again. Mary is restored to life and love and joy. It is another resurrection moment, for that is the kind of God God is.

11

The Great Fifty Days

Season

Lent, with its '40 days', gives way to Easter with its 50 days, often called the 'Great Fifty Days' – and this time the number of days is accurate. Forty days from Easter Day brings us to Ascension Day and ten more to the Day of Pentecost. But the special character of these 50 days is far less understood in most church communities than the 40 days of Lent. Churches generally mark Lent out as a significant penitential season, with its own ethos and character, and do not at some stage let it fade away and relapse into treating it as 'ordinary time'. But that is exactly what many of them do with Eastertide. By the Second Sunday of Easter the paschal character is sometimes being lost. By the Sixth Sunday any thought of a season of the resurrection has disappeared. This is very regrettable. A sustained period of Easter joy in which to explore the 'paschal mystery' of Christ's resurrection and ascension and the gift of the Holy Spirit has great potential for good worship and effective mission. The Great Fifty Days need, where they have been lost, to be reclaimed. As *Times and Seasons* puts it:

> The Great Fifty Days of Eastertide form a single festival period in which the tone of joy created at the Easter Vigil is sustained through the following seven weeks, and the Church celebrates the gloriously risen Christ. (p. 427)

The Book of Common Prayer has, in this respect, something to answer for. First of all it names the Sundays of the season as Sundays 'after Easter' and that term has allowed people to feel that Easter is over when it has in reality only just begun. *Common Worship* very firmly speaks of Sundays 'of Easter' to underline this, though it leads to a little confusion when holding the two calendars together for the First Sunday 'after Easter' is, of course, the Second Sunday 'of Easter'. The Book of Common Prayer adds to this impression by ordering the Easter preface at the Eucharist for just eight days (the old idea of an 'octave' for major feasts), followed by more than four weeks of no proper preface, then an eight-day preface for the Ascension and a seven-day one for Whitsun, as if there were three distinct seasons. The Book of Common Prayer collects and readings for Holy Communion also cease to have a paschal resonance once the Second Sunday after Easter has been passed. Eastertide seems to fade almost as quickly as the Easter flowers. Not so *Common Worship* and *Times and Seasons* with 50 days of sustained joy and celebration, seasonal texts and a sense of development towards the Day of Pentecost.

Scripture

It is important to understand that in terms of the Gospels we are dealing with two Easter chronologies and that the Christian year chooses to go with the Lukan chronology. If we follow Luke, in his Gospel and in the Acts of the Apostles, the Easter event is spread out over 50 days. That is how we celebrate it with a 50-day Easter season, taking in Ascension Day on the way, with Pentecost at the end. In Luke's chronology, the Lord is raised from the dead on Easter Day, and for a period of some 40 days appears and disappears, coming and going, revealing himself to his followers, until a particular day, 40 days on, when he is taken from them, as far as bodily manifestations are concerned, in an event we call the ascension, and which Luke pictures as a physical departure from the earth (Acts 1.6–11). Then, after ten days of expectant waiting, comes Pentecost, and the sudden and dramatic outpouring of the Holy Spirit in wind and flame (Acts 2.1–36). The account in Luke's Gospel is silent about the days after the resurrection and it is Acts that gives us the 40 days:

> In the first book, Theophilus, I wrote about all that Jesus did and taught from the beginning until the day when he was taken up to heaven, after giving instructions through the Holy Spirit to the apostles whom he had chosen. After his suffering he presented himself alive to them by many convincing proofs, appearing to them over the course of forty days and speaking about the kingdom of God. (Acts 1.1–3)

To an extent the apostle Paul reflects the Lukan approach of appearances over a period of time when he writes to the Christians at Corinth:

> For I handed on to you as of first importance what I in turn had received: that Christ died for our sins in accordance with the scriptures, and that he was buried, and that he was raised on the third day in accordance with the scriptures, and that he appeared to Cephas, then to the twelve. Then he appeared to more than five hundred brothers and sisters at one time, most of whom are still alive, though some have died. Then he appeared to James, then to all the apostles. Last of all, as to someone untimely born, he appeared also to me. (1 Corinthians 15.3–8)

John's chronology is different. In the Fourth Gospel Jesus is raised from the dead and on that same day says to Mary Magdalene,

> Do not hold on to me, because I have not yet ascended to the Father. But go to my brothers and say to them, 'I am ascending to my Father and your Father, to my God and your God.' (John 20.17)

Then a little later on the same day in the upper room he is breathing on his disciples and saying, 'Receive the Holy Spirit' (John 20.22), so that Pentecost is suddenly not 50 days on, but there on Easter night. Eight days later he, who has said earlier, 'Do not hold on to me, because I have not yet ascended,' says to Thomas, 'Reach out your hand and put it in my side' (John 20.27). Mary Magdalene was not to touch him, but now Thomas is invited to do so. It seems that for John ascending is not a physical thing, but a kind of internal spiritual experience that has been going on inside Jesus as part of the business of being raised from the dead. By the time he is talking to Thomas he has, spiritually, ascended and has given the Spirit. It is as if resurrection, ascension and the giving of the Spirit are a single event.

Matthew's chronology is more like that of the Fourth Gospel. We tend to read his account through Lukan eyes and therefore to assume that, when Jesus came to the 11 disciples on the mountain to which he had directed them and there gave them the commission with which his Gospel ends, this is an event 40 days on, just as Luke makes it. But Matthew says nothing to suggest this. He moves straight from his account of the guards accepting a bribe to say that the disciples' had stolen the body of Jesus to the scene with the 11 on the mountain (Matthew 28.11–20). Inasmuch as this is the ascension, it follows straight on from the resurrection. Matthew, of course, does not record a Pentecost event.

How are we to reconcile these two quite different chronologies? The answer is that we cannot and we shall never know which of them is historically the more accurate. Some would say that Luke's spreading the story out over 50 days is the more accurate, because Luke was writing earlier and John is always better as a theologian reflecting on the truth than as a historian reporting the facts. On that argument John has brought together these three events – resurrection, ascension and the coming of the Spirit – in order to show us that they belong together, three aspects of one mystery, the Easter event. He is not, on this argument, interested in accurate chronology; he is making an important theological point.

Others see it the other way round. The truth, they would say, is that the total Easter event was in a single moment, so to speak, the risen ascending Lord giving the Spirit, all at Easter; but that it was, in a sense, too much to take in and so the Church, beginning with Luke, spread it out over 50 days, so as to have space to take in the mystery, one event after another, one truth after another, till it was all assimilated. On that argument, John is the more accurate, but Luke is the better teacher, helping us to hear the stories and to receive the truth and make them our own. And that is indeed exactly what we do through the seven weeks from Easter to Pentecost if we celebrate the Great Fifty Days.

The lectionary through Eastertide focuses principally on the Acts of the Apostles and on the Fourth Gospel. Following the *Revised Common Lectionary* the *Common Worship* principal service lectionary expects the Acts of the Apostles, rather than a passage from the Hebrew Scriptures, to be read as the first reading each Sunday. It is a liturgical practice that goes back at least to Augustine in the fifth century and has been part of the Ambrosian and Hispanic rites in the West, as well as Eastern rites. Acts is the obvious book to read in the weeks of Easter, partly because so many of the speeches within it testify to the resurrection of the Lord and partly because it describes the phenomenal growth of the Church in the power of the Easter/ Pentecost experience. Where a church has only one reading before the Gospel, it is the Acts passage that is the priority. When there is a second reading it is from 1 Peter (in Year A), the letters of John (in Year B) and Revelation (in Year C). The purpose of this selection

is to complement the Acts narrative of the formation and growth of the resurrection community with a theological commentary on the character of its inner life, namely, its mutual love, and its life of praise in anticipation of the fulfilment of the kingdom. (*The Revised Common Lectionary*, p. 14)

Recognizing that there is sometimes a need for a reading from the Old Testament (when the lectionary is used with Morning or Evening Prayer) a sequence drawn from the Vigil readings of the Easter Liturgy is provided, but these are not intended for the Eucharist or ever to supersede the Acts readings.

The Gospel readings for the first three Sundays of Easter tell the resurrection stories. The two appearances in the upper room (John 20.19–31) are heard every year on the Second Sunday. On the Third Sunday Year A tells the Emmaus story (Luke 24.13–35), Year B Luke's account of the appearance to all the disciples (Luke 24.36b–48) and Year C John's account of the fishing expedition and the lakeside breakfast (John 21.1–19). After that the Gospel readings stay with John in all three years and, beginning with three passages over the three years from John 10 regarding Jesus as the Good Shepherd, with its own paschal flavour, then turn to the Farewell Discourses and draw from John 13, 14 and 15 passages that interact with the other readings of the day and prepare the ground for the ascension and for the giving of the Spirit. But the move to these Johannine passages is not intended to mark a shift away from resurrection texts through the service. The Great Fifty Days continue with their alleluias and texts that resonate with the resurrection stories.

Candle, Font and Garden

Alongside this consistent staying with the Easter themes there should be a continuing focus on the Easter artefacts in the church. The first is the Easter Candle on its stand, the sign of the presence of the Risen Lord, placed prominently throughout the Easter season, lit at every service, and moved to the font after the Day of Pentecost, used at every baptism through the year and brought back from the font only at funerals where it stands near the coffin, a reminder of the Christian's dying and rising with Christ. But that is all to anticipate what happens at the end of the season. For the Fifty Days it stands in a prominent position, probably near the lectern or the altar table, perhaps enhanced by flowers, though it is important to remember that the flowers are there to honour the Candle, not the Candle to enhance a flower arrangement!

The second artefact is the font. Although it is always in the church and ought always to have its own space and not become simply a repository for flowers or even notice sheets, in Eastertide, with all its baptismal associations, it is helpful to highlight it, perhaps by lighting, perhaps by flowers, certainly by keeping it filled with water, perhaps by saying the Prayers of Penitence throughout the season at the font and sprinkling the congregation with water from it at the Absolution.

The third is an Easter Garden. There is no garden in the traditional liturgical ceremonies of Easter, but it has become a well-established Anglican practice to make such a garden. The larger it can be the better; something on a tea tray is too domestic. Most important is a tomb, with a great stone rolled away and linen cloths within the tomb. But there may also be shrubs and flowers and there may be the figures of the disciples, men and women, at the tomb. In the distance on a hill there may be three empty crosses. Here is an opportunity for creativity in making something striking that captures the Easter good news. To pause at the Easter Garden during a processional entry during Eastertide and to say a prayer is appropriate. *Times and Seasons* provides material, including a prayer to bless the garden on Easter Day. The Easter Garden might, of course, be outside the building. Like any other garden, it needs watering and other garden maintenance if it is to remain fresh till Ascension Day or Pentecost.

Texts

A word should be said about the Easter word – Alleluia. Silent through Lent, alleluia belongs to every other season of the year, especially in heralding the Gospel reading, but it is particularly the Easter word. Augustine is credited with saying, 'We are the Easter people and alleluia is our song.' Sometimes it will be spoken, but more often it needs to be sung. Many hymn books now provide musical alleluias, whether from Taizé, South Africa, Iona or Rome, and every congregation should have one in its repertoire, ready to use at set times in the liturgy or more spontaneously on Easter Day and through the season till Pentecost. In particular the Easter Acclamation, the Easter Invitation to Communion and the Easter Dismissal, each with their alleluias, should always be used through the Easter season. Alleluia can be added to other sentences in the liturgy. The alleluia hymns and songs have a special quality and should continue through the season, especially later in Eastertide when the Gospel readings have moved on from accounts of the empty tomb and the resurrection appearances and it is the hymns and songs that retell and reinforce the story.

The Easter Acclamation – *Alleluia. Christ is risen.* **He is risen indeed. Alleluia.** – does not need to be restricted to the moment after the opening greeting. It can certainly be used after the Gospel, at the beginning or end of the sermon and before the blessing, or indeed at any point spontaneously that the worship leader thinks appropriate.

The special texts of Easter go beyond those found in the *Common Worship* Eucharist with their alleluias. *Times and Seasons* (pp. 428ff.) includes a rich provision of Eastertide prayers of penitence and intercession and an extended dismissal rite. But there are four other more substantial texts and it is worth exploring where they might be used in the course of the Great Fifty Days.

The first is the text known as the 'Easter Anthems', a compilation drawn from Romans and 1 Corinthians, which the Book of Common Prayer ordered for use at Morning Prayer on Easter Morning, but which is now encouraged daily at Morning Prayer from Easter to Ascension (*Common Worship, Daily Prayer*, p. 634). It is a fine text, whether spoken or sung, and is worthy of being used at times other than Morning Prayer. Its structure is such that it is particularly effective where the leader speaks the first half of each verse, with the congregation responding with the second half.

The second is another text to be found in *Common Worship, Daily Prayer* (p. 640). This is *Victimae Paschali*, the Easter Sequence in use from its composition by Wipo of Burgundy in the eleventh century. It is a dialogue text that deserves to be better known and incorporated into Easter worship, particularly effective in its latter part that draws on the experience of Mary Magdalene.

Speak, Mary, friend of Christ,
what did you see on sorrow's road?
Tell us your story.
I saw the tomb of the living Christ.
I saw his resurrection glory.
I saw the witnessing angels.
I saw the head-cloth and the shroud.
Christ my hope has risen,
and goes before his own to Galilee.
Trust Mary, believers,
for only she has truth to tell,
unlike the falsifying crowd
of rumour-makers and deceivers.
We know that Christ is truly risen,
defeating death and hell's dark thrall,
so conquering king,
have mercy on us all.
Alleluia.

Almost credal, it can serve, as the hymns that tell the Easter story do, to reinforce the good news of the resurrection in Eastertide services at which the accounts of the resurrection are not being read.

The third is Eric Milner-White's beautiful Thanksgiving for the Resurrection (*Times and Seasons*, pp. 421ff.). It is in four parts, not all of which need to be used on every occasion. *Times and Seasons* suggests that it might be used between the Easter Acclamation and the Gloria at the Eucharist, but it is equally suitable in a non-eucharistic liturgy, especially as it can provide the thanksgiving element that can sometimes be missing in such a service. It could be sung in procession and the second part is particularly suitable in procession to the font at an Eastertide baptism.

The fourth paschal text is a complete service of its own, a contemporary series of Stations of the Resurrection to parallel the traditional Stations of the Cross. *Times and Seasons* describes these stations as a complementary devotion emerging 'in the latter part of the twentieth century, possibly from the Iberian Peninsula', though another source traces the origin to Father Sabino Palumbieri in Rome. These Stations of the Resurrection are designed to be used like the traditional Stations of the Cross, with a Scripture reading, space for meditation or reflection and prayer at each station. Although some versions have 14 stations, matching the number of the traditional stations, others have more and the *Times and Seasons* version has 19, increasing the number of stations that relate to resurrection appearances, concluding with the appearance to Paul on the Damascus Road. The expectation is that the Stations will normally involve movement around the building (or in the open air) with the nature of a pilgrimage. *Times and Seasons* devotes nearly 30 pages to this innovative liturgy (pp. 443ff.), with a Gathering and a Conclusion and texts for each of the 19 stations. What needs to follow is the commissioning of paintings or other artwork to illustrate the Easter journey. As with the traditional stations, one can be selective in how many and which stations to use on any given occasion.

Ascension Day

The momentum of Eastertide brings us, after 40 days, to Ascension Day, always a Thursday and never transferred to the following Sunday, though in Year A the Acts of the Apostles account of the ascension (Acts 1.6–11) forms part of the first reading on that Sunday. On Ascension Day both of Luke's accounts, in Acts and in his Gospel, are appointed for the principal service. The Acts reading has some parting words from Jesus with the promise of the Holy Spirit and the commission to be his witnesses 'in Jerusalem, in all Judea and Samaria, and to the ends of the earth'. As the disciples watch, Jesus is lifted up and a cloud takes him out of their sight (Acts 1.8–9). The Gospel says it more simply.

> He led them out as far as Bethany, and lifting up his hands, he blessed them. While he was blessing them, he withdrew from them and was carried up into heaven. And they worshipped him, and returned to Jerusalem with great joy; and they were continually in the temple blessing God. (Luke 24.50–53)

Luke is trying to describe the indescribable. Perhaps Matthew, who has the commission but not the withdrawal and who indeed has Jesus speak of his being with them 'to the end of the age', is on safer ground. John too, for whom ascension seems to be a more internal spiritual process, does not have to try to describe how Jesus withdraws from the earth. What is it that the Church celebrates on Ascension Day? Certainly not the end of Easter. Certainly not the Divine Absence. Both Matthew and Luke speak of the disciples 'worshipping' Jesus. It is a word that the Gospels do not often use about their relationship with Jesus. It is always at a moment of revelation, a moment when suddenly they understand something more deeply than before, nearly always a moment when they know more clearly who he is. It is because they understand at last who he is that they no longer need his physical presence coming and going and that they can worship and be full of joy. The ascension is like another key piece fitted into the jigsaw, the penultimate piece, and now they can focus on looking for the one piece that still needs to be put in place. In a sense the ascension is the last of the resurrection appearances (though Paul thinks of his conversion as another one). It is an appearance that no longer needs to deal with sorrow, as with Mary Magdalene, or with guilt, as with Peter, or with doubt, as with Thomas. Now it can be all blessing, commission, joy and completion, though a completion that leaves us with the wonderful paradox that he who has returned to the Father is with us to the end of time.

There is no special liturgical action associated with Ascension Day. There used to be one, when the custom was to extinguish the Paschal Candle for the last time after the reading of the Gospel on Ascension Day. That seemed to say something like 'Now you see him, now you don't.' But the Candle continues to be lit till Pentecost, partly because Easter is not over, but principally because the ascended Lord is still among his people as he promised even if the physical appearances have ended.

There is no special liturgical action, but *Times and Seasons* does provide a special eucharistic liturgy (pp. 470ff.). Because it is still Easter some features do not change – the Easter Acclamation, the Easter Invitation to Communion, the Easter Dismissal. But there are new and additional texts to capture the story and meaning of the day. Not just the Easter Acclamation, but also

God has gone up with a shout,
the Lord with the sound of the trumpet.

Not only the Easter Invitation to Communion, but an alternative.

I heard the voice of a great multitude crying, Alleluia.
The Lord our God has entered into his kingdom.
Blessed are those who are called to the supper of the Lamb.
Alleluia.

Not just the Easter Dismissal but

Waiting expectantly for the promised Holy Spirit,
go in the peace of Christ. Alleluia, alleluia.
Thanks be to God. Alleluia, alleluia.

There are naturally special texts for the Intercession, the Peace, the Eucharistic Preface and the Blessing. But there are also special features at the beginning and the end of the service. At the beginning there is a scripted introduction to the service setting the scene, followed immediately by the reading from Acts before the singing of the *Gloria*. Moving this reading from its place in the Liturgy of the Word into the Gathering enables it to spell out what Ascension Day celebrates and to stamp that story on the service from the beginning.

The extended Dismissal has a different function. It is to begin to move us on to what follows and to prepare for Pentecost. Once the Prayers after Communion have been said, three more verses of Acts 1 (1.12, 13a and 14) are read with their account of Mary and the disciples and brothers of Jesus, after the ascension, praying in the upper room and awaiting the promised Spirit. It leads into a Responsory with its repeated refrain, 'Make us ready for your coming Spirit', before the Blessing and Dismissal. It is another of those transition points when the liturgy changes direction, as on Palm Sunday and Maundy Thursday. The Eucharist has celebrated the return of Jesus to the Father. The Dismissal moves the focus firmly to prayerful waiting for the Spirit, in other words towards Pentecost. Such an end to Ascension Day worship would also make sense at a non-eucharistic service. It is with the Holy Spirit and with Pentecost that the final chapter engages.

Pentecost

The Nine Days

There is no time in the Christian year where there is more confusion than around the Day of Pentecost. The difficulty arises from there being two quite different understandings. Those whose understanding of the calendar was shaped by The Book of Common Prayer think of a brief season of the Ascension, ten days after Easter is over, followed by a new season, Whitsun, beginning on Whitsunday and lasting just a week, with Trinity Sunday following a week after Whitsunday.

But the *Common Worship* calendar, reflecting both an older tradition and the contemporary practice of other Christian churches, understands it differently. It doesn't understand Whitsunday/Pentecost as a season at all, but as the last day of Easter, and it doesn't understand the nine days between Ascension Day and Pentecost as an Ascension season, but as part of Easter, albeit a part with a special emphasis on the Holy Spirit. It sees the return to 'ordinary time' as happening on what we used to call Whit Monday, for the Great Fifty Days have reached their climax and their end on the Day of Pentecost. Of course there is a need as part of the cycle of the Christian year to explore and celebrate the place of the Holy Spirit, but it is in the nine days that lead to Pentecost, not in the six days after Pentecost, which is why *Common Worship* does not expect Pentecost material to be used on the days after the Day of Pentecost and even provides a different Collect and Post Communion for the weekdays that follow. This understanding

of Pentecost is well expressed in the Post Communion Prayer
for the Day of Pentecost, which begins:

> Faithful God, who fulfilled the promises of Easter by sending
> us your Holy Spirit and opening to every race and nation the
> way of life eternal. . . (*Common Worship*, p. 405)

Having followed the Lukan chronology, we are reminded at
Pentecost of the Johannine understanding that resurrection and
Holy Spirit, Easter and Pentecost, belong together. This has
implications for the days between Ascension Day and Pentecost.
The *Common Worship* calendar states: 'From Friday after
Ascension Day begin the nine days of prayer before Pentecost.'
People may claim those nine days (or 'novena') for prayers
for unity or prayers for mission, but fundamentally they are
prayers waiting expectantly for the Holy Spirit. The key prayer
is 'Come, Holy Spirit.' These days are intended to reflect liturgically what is described in the Book of Acts in relation to the
first Ascension Day and the days that followed it.

> While staying with them, [Jesus] ordered them not to leave
> Jerusalem, but to wait there for the promise of the Father.
> 'This', he said, 'is what you have heard from me; for John
> baptized with water, but you will be baptized with the Holy
> Spirit not many days from now.' (Acts 1.4–5)

> When they had entered the city, they went to the room upstairs
> where they were staying, Peter, and John, and James, and
> Andrew, Philip and Thomas, Bartholomew and Matthew,
> James son of Alphaeus, and Simon the Zealot, and Judas
> son of James. All these were constantly devoting themselves
> to prayer, together with certain women, including Mary the
> mother of Jesus, as well as his brothers. (Acts 1.13–14)

It is not that, once Ascension Day is over, it is entirely forgotten
and Pentecost has taken over, because clearly the Ascension and

the Coming of the Spirit are closely linked. It is the particular function of the Seventh Sunday of Easter, falling between the Ascension and Pentecost, and with its readings from Acts, to hold the two together, which it does beautifully in the Collect for the Day, which dates from the First Prayer Book of 1549.

> O God the King of glory,
> you have exalted your only Son Jesus Christ
> with great triumph to your kingdom in heaven:
> we beseech you, leave us not comfortless,
> but send your Holy Spirit to strengthen us
> and exalt us to the place
> where our Saviour Christ is gone before,
> who is alive and reigns with you,
> in the unity of the Holy Spirit,
> one God, now and for ever.
> (*Common Worship*, p. 404)

It has implications for the hymns and songs of this Sunday and for the task of the preacher. The service may begin with the Ascension theme, but, by the end, people need to be moving into a prayerful mood that looks for the coming of the Spirit. Hymns and songs that in the past have been thought to belong only to the Day of Pentecost, especially those that ask the Spirit to come, are absolutely appropriate on this Sixth Sunday of Easter.

The reason for this change is not just a liturgical nicety or tidying up. It is in order that Pentecost itself may be more than simply the commemoration of a historical event. We say or sing 'Come, Holy Spirit' in the days before Pentecost not simply to prepare us to celebrate the event described in Acts 2, but to open our hearts for a fresh outpouring of the Holy Spirit on us as we approach and celebrate the feast. Just as at Advent the Church prays 'Come, Lord Jesus', not just in relation to a birth at Bethlehem, but in the confident hope of a coming again at the end of time, so in these final days of Easter the

Church prays 'Come, Holy Spirit', not just in relation to what happened in the upper room, but in expectation of what can happen today.

Although Eastertide continues, there is a different set of Invitation to Confession, Gospel Alleluia, Introduction to the Peace, Eucharistic Preface and Blessing provided for these days in *Common Worship* (pp. 320f.), and *Common Worship, Daily Prayer* has different forms of Morning and Evening Prayer (pp. 278ff.). There is also a series of lectionary readings focusing on the Holy Spirit for use morning or evening on the eight weekdays in preparation for the Day of Pentecost.

Day 1	Ex. 35.30—36.1	&	Gal. 5.13–end
Day 2	Num. 11.16–17,24–29	&	1 Cor. 2
Day 3	Num. 27.15–end	&	1 Cor. 3
Day 4	1 Sam. 10.1–10	&	1 Cor. 12.1–13
Day 5	1 Kings 19.1–18	&	Matt. 3.13–end
Day 6	Ezek. 11.14–20	&	Matt. 9.35—10.20
Day 7	Ezek. 36.22–28	&	Matt. 12.22–32
Day 8	Micah 3.1–8	&	Eph. 6.10–20

But this material will impact only on those who share in Morning and Evening Prayer. There is a case for a special Vigil Service either on Pentecost Eve or one of the earlier days in that week, to which more people would come. Some of the readings above would provide for a sequence of Scripture, with perhaps John 7.37–39 as the Gospel reading. For those wanting to include canticles, the Song of the Lord's Anointed, the Song of Ezekiel, the Song of Tobit, the Song of Judith and the Song of Wisdom would be suitable, as would the Song of Ephrem and the Sequence, *Veni Sancte Spiritus*, all of which are to be found in *Common Worship, Daily Prayer* (pp. 586ff.). But in many places the need will be for hymns, songs and chants. *Ancient & Modern* has a particularly fine collection of new hymns honouring the Holy Spirit and there is also a good variety of chants, including John Bell's 'Come, Holy Spirit' (*A&M* 240), Daniel

Iverson's 'Spirit of the living God' (*A&M* 263), the Taizé chant *Veni Sancte Spiritus* (*A&M* 266) and Peter Nardone's 'Veni, veni' (*A&M* 267). The most important element of such a Vigil is a silent and expectant waiting.

The Day of Pentecost

The last day of Easter is like the last piece put into the jig-saw. With the coming of the promised Holy Spirit upon the Christian community the paschal mystery is complete. Christ has died, has been raised and has ascended and now the Father has sent the Spirit. We can see the whole picture and how it all fits together. Clearly the key text is Acts 2.

> When the day of Pentecost had come, they were all together in one place. And suddenly from heaven there came a sound like the rush of a violent wind, and it filled the entire house where they were sitting. Divided tongues, as of fire, appeared among them, and a tongue rested on each of them. All of them were filled with the Holy Spirit and began to speak in other languages, as the Spirit gave them ability. (Acts 2.1–4)

People from all over the known world heard them and understood them, Peter spoke powerfully and many came to faith. The Acts story is read at the principal service every year, but the use of John 20.19–23 in Year A is a reminder of the Fourth Gospel's picture of the Spirit given seven weeks earlier on Easter evening.

It is important to be careful about how we speak of the Holy Spirit at Pentecost. This was the coming of the Holy Spirit upon the Christian community, but it was not the first experience of the Holy Spirit as if there had been no Holy Spirit before. Genesis speaks of the Spirit hovering over the waters when the world was created (Genesis 1.2). The Holy Spirit overshadowed Mary at the annunciation (Luke 1.35), inspired Elizabeth when Mary visited her (Luke 1.41) and came upon Jesus at his baptism (Luke 3.22). The Spirit of God fills the whole world, but what we celebrate on the Day of Pentecost is the coming of the Spirit upon the Christian community, which is why it is sometimes called 'the birthday of the Church', and what we yearn for is a fresh outpouring of the Spirit on the Church and on Christian people today.

Times and Seasons provides a complete eucharistic liturgy for the Day of Pentecost (pp. 491ff.). The church building will still be dressed for Easter, but the liturgical colour is red for the Spirit. Red for the tongues of flame – red on the vestments, red on the hangings, maybe red banners, maybe the congregation invited to wear red too. What was written above about possible hymns, songs and chants for the nine days before applies also to Pentecost itself. As with other services, much of the material within this liturgy will transfer to a non-eucharistic context. The pattern for Pentecost is much as for the Ascension Day liturgy described in the last chapter, though this time there is a new liturgical action. Because it is still Easter some features do not change – the Easter Acclamation, the Easter Invitation to Communion, the Easter Dismissal. There are naturally special texts for the Intercession, the Peace, the Eucharistic Preface and the Blessing.

The Solemn Blessing (p. 502), holding together creation, annunciation, resurrection and Pentecost, reinforces the truth that the Holy Spirit is not new at Pentecost, but has always been the agent of God's activity.

May the Spirit,
who hovered over the waters when the world was created,
breathe into you the life he gives. **Amen.**

May the Spirit,
who overshadowed the Virgin
when the eternal Son came among us,
make you joyful in the service of the Lord. **Amen.**

May the Spirit,
who set the Church on fire upon the day of Pentecost,
bring the world alive with the love of the risen Christ. **Amen.**

But, more fundamentally, there are also special features at the beginning and the end of the service. At the beginning there is a scripted introduction setting the scene, a kind of recapitulation of the Easter season now coming to its end. There follows a Responsory to the Holy Spirit, which mirrors the one with which the Ascension Day liturgy ended. The repeated response is 'Fill us with your Spirit'. As on Ascension Day this leads into the Acts reading, moved from its usual place in the Liturgy of the Word to stamp the Pentecost story on the service from the beginning. However, today it leads, not (yet) into the Gloria, but into what it calls 'Prayer for Personal Renewal'. It is an invitation to all who wish to do so, children as well as adults, to come forward to be anointed with the oil of chrism – chrism with its association with the gift of the Spirit in baptism, confirmation and ordination and therefore with the Christian's sense of calling and commission. The service allows for the blessing of oil and provides a text, but much better that the oil blessed by the bishop on Maundy Thursday and brought back to the local community should be used. Traditionally the oil of chrism is used only by ordained ministers, but if the number of people present require it lay people might need to share in this ministry. Indeed in places where there are 'ministry teams' who offer healing ministry on a regular basis they are the obvious people to use on this occasion. There is no text provided for what the minister says to each person as they are anointed. Clearly this could be done silently, but on the Day of Pentecost a reference to the Spirit would seem right, perhaps 'May the Holy Spirit fill you with the life of the risen Christ.' A note encourages appropriate singing while the anointing is taking place.

There is an issue about whether such an anointing should be sprung on people without warning. Traditionally anointing with oil has been a solemn act for which people would be prepared. If this is to be included in the Pentecost service there ought to have been some teaching about it (for it is an innovation) and some reference to it in church notices, so that people have the opportunity to come ready and open for this ministry.

When all who wish to have been anointed, the Eucharist continues with the Gloria and is then on a familiar route through until after the distribution of Holy Communion. A note permits the insertion of Prayers of Penitence before the Peace, but the anointing ought to be understood as encompassing a sense of penitence and forgiveness and this is a service in some danger of being too long. For there is another innovation to come.

How is this Easter season to be brought to a proper end? It began with the lighting of the Easter Candle and its procession through the church. There is much to be said for using the Candle to mark the end of the season, though not by blowing it out as if Jesus has gone. The liturgy provides for a minister to say a prayer at the Candle to bless the light and for everyone to have candles that are now lit from the Easter Candle. If the geography of the church permits, there might then be a movement, led by a minister carrying the Easter Candle, to the font. Gathered at the font (or turning towards it) and holding their lighted candles, the members of the congregation are asked in a 'Commissioning' text to dare to grow together in love, to share riches and minister to each other, to pray for one another and 'to carry the light of Christ into the world's dark places', each question inviting a strong 'We will'. The rubrics then encourage a move outside for the Solemn Blessing and the Dismissal. There is a case for the Commissioning also to be outside, rather than at the font. If the Easter Candle and the other candles are blown out by the wind, that is no matter – the light of the Risen Christ and the flame of the Holy Spirit no longer need a Candle. Through the paschal mystery they are within the people who have moved outside because it is outside the church building that by the power of the Spirit they need to make Christ known.

If there is only one service in the church on Pentecost this ending will obviously happen at the end of that service. But if there is a later service, an Evening Prayer for instance or something less formal, there is clearly a case for keeping this Dismissal rite with the Candle and the Commissioning for the end of that later service. For the Great Fifty Days come to an end with the last alleluia of the last service of the Day of Pentecost. To my mind the best of all hymns for the end of that final service is 'We have a gospel to proclaim' (*A&M* 507), with its recapitulation of resurrection, ascension and Pentecost within the context of a call to evangelism – 'We have a gospel to proclaim.'

After Pentecost

By next day 'ordinary time' has returned. The liturgical colour is green. The Easter Candle has been moved to stand by the font for use at baptism, though brought to stand next to the coffin at funerals. The Easter Garden has gone too. The alleluias will not cease until the following Lent, but there will be fewer of them. There is no need to empty the font of water, though the water will need renewing regularly. Encouraging people to dip their hand in it every time they come into the church would put them in mind not only of their baptism, but also of their participation in the life-changing liturgies of Lent, Holy Week and Easter.

Last words

The plea of this book has been to make connections. Isn't what happened to Peter in Holy Week and at Easter just the kind of experience we have in our own lives and see in others around us? Is not the Mary Magdalene story mirrored in our own story too? And mirrored not just once, but repeatedly? It is the divine pattern, by the power of the Holy Spirit to bring healing out of brokenness, light out of darkness, joy out of despair, and sometimes the language of 'life out of death' seems appropriate too.

Much of the time that divine activity of renewing and refreshing goes on so secretly that we hardly notice that God is at work, always sowing the seeds of resurrection and always ensuring new life sees the light of day. But sometimes there are significant moments when we can sense that the resurrecting God is acting upon us. Sometimes it is sufficiently transformational that others can see it too, as it was on the Day of Pentecost.

Over the years I have often looked back to a particular time when I sensed the resurrecting God at work in my own life in a way that was transformational. The details are unimportant. Like many young people I had been wounded by a love affair that had gone wrong and ended badly. I remember living through what seemed an eternity (I think just a few weeks in reality, maybe something like 40 days and 40 nights) working slowly, patiently, with grief, but being aware that God also was working slowly, patiently, reliably and lovingly with me, and with my grief. I sensed that, though I was in a kind of tunnel, there would be light at the end of it. And when, through that patient, reliable loving of God, I emerged, I might have said simply 'I feel better now' or 'I've got over it' or 'I am moving on', all of which would have been a quite adequate way of putting it. But what I did find myself saying, at least to myself, was 'this is what resurrection is all about'. This is the resurrecting God who loves us back into life. I have been clear about resurrection ever since. What God did in Jesus, God does in you and me. I learned that for myself some 40 years ago and, although it is a truth that never leaves me, more recently I have found myself learning it, the Christ-like way, again. The way of Christ-likeness is always a path walked with a Risen Lord who does not hide his wounds.

If I urge people and communities to have a deeper, richer and more fulfilling experience of the 40 days of Lent, of Holy

Week and of the Great Fifty Days of Easter, it is only that they may have the opportunity to be transformed by the experience. If I spend time and energy showing how the liturgy of Holy Week and Eastertide needs thinking through theologically and pastorally, with a care for detail that can make it an agent of change, it is only that people and communities may become more alive, more Christ-like and more full of the grace of the resurrecting God.

References and Further Reading

Alternative Service Book 1980, 1980, Church House Publishing, London.

Ancient & Modern: Hymns and Songs for Refreshing Worship, 2013, Hymns Ancient & Modern Ltd, Norwich.

Bradshaw, Paul and Maxwell Johnson, 2011, *The Origins of Feasts, Fasts and Seasons in Early Christianity*, SPCK, London.

Common Worship: Services and Prayers for the Church of England, 2000, Church House Publishing, London.

Common Worship, Daily Prayer, 2005, London, Church House Publishing.

Common Worship, Times and Seasons, 2006, Church House Publishing, London.

Gordon-Taylor, Benjamin and Simon Jones, 2009, *Celebrating Christ's Victory*, SPCK, London.

The Hymnal, 1982, Church Hymnal Corp., New York.

The Hymnal of the Protestant Episcopal Church in the United States of America, 1940, Church Pension Fund, New York.

Hymns for Prayer and Praise, 1996, Canterbury Press, Norwich.

Hymns Old and New: One Church, One Faith, One Lord, 2004, Kevin Mayhew Limited, Stowmarket.

Lent, Holy Week, Easter, 1986, Church House Publishing, Cambridge University Press and SPCK, London.

The New English Hymnal, 1986, Canterbury Press, Norwich.

New Patterns for Worship, 2002, Church House Publishing, London.

Perham, Michael, 1998, *The Sorrowful Way*, SPCK, London.

Perham, Michael and Kenneth Stevenson, 2013, *Waiting for the Risen Christ: Commentary on Lent, Holy Week, Easter – Services and Prayers*, SPCK, London.

The Revised Common Lectionary, 1992, Canterbury Press, Norwich.

Wilkinson, John, 1999, *Egeria's Travels*, Arris and Phillips, Oxford.

Williams, Dick, 1969, *Godthoughts*, Falcon, London.

Index of Bible References

Index of Names and Subjects

Whitsunday *see* Pentecost
Wigmore, Paul 53
wilderness *see* desert
Williams, Dick 19
wine 3, 31, 36, 57–8, 60, 70, 73,
   89–92, 103

Wipo of Burgundy 132
Woollcombe, Kenneth 3
Wren Brian 65
Wright, Ralph 85